By Divine Instruction

Lessons in Metaphysical Healing

A guided healing handbook

Ann M Basili

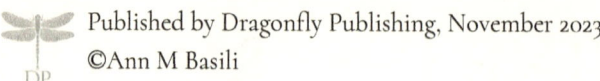 Published by Dragonfly Publishing, November 2023
©Ann M Basili

This book is copyright. Apart from any fair dealing for the purpose of private study, research, criticism or review, as permitted under the Copyright Act, no part may be reproduced by any process without written permission from the publisher.

The author acknowledges the trademark status and trademark owners of various products referenced in this work, which have been used without permission. The publication/use of these trademarks is not authorised, associated with, or sponsored by the trademark owners.

Because of the dynamic nature of the Internet, any web addresses or links contained in this book may have changed since publication and may no longer be valid. The views expressed in this work are solely those of the author(s) and do not necessarily reflect the views of the publisher and the publisher hereby disclaims any responsibility for them.

 A catalogue record for this work is available from the National Library of Australia

Edited by Michelle E. Smith

ISBN(sc): 978-0-6458702-0-6
ISBN(e): 978-0-6458702-1-3

Dedications

To my mother, who carried the last traces of our ancient Egyptian culture's wisdom and knowledge.

I am one of the last in our genetic line of Pharaonic "pure bloods", the mysteries and knowledge of which I am only now waking up to. The responsibility for which I must now share.

Contents

Dedications

Preface ~ In the Beginning was the Word ~

Introduction ~ About the Book ~
   ~ Self-Healing Is the New Paradigm

Part I ~ About Me ~
   ~ Who Am I? ~ 1
   ~ Spiritual and Healing Evolution ~ 8

Part II ~ The Illness ~
   ~ The Mystery Illness ~ 17

Part III ~ Committing to Yourself and Your Body ~
   ~ Self-Commitments ~ 25
   ~ The Ten Self-Commitments ~ 26
   ~ Self-Commitment No. 1 ~ *Commitment to My Body - Do I Accept and Love This Body?* 27
   ~ Self-Commitment No. 2 ~ *The Power of a Positive Mind - Positive Thoughts and Speech* 30
   ~ Self-Commitment No. 3 ~ *Do You Believe? Challenging and Replacing Limiting Beliefs* 34
   ~ Self-Commitment No. 4 ~ *No Fear - Releasing Any Fear of the Unknown* 39
   ~ Self-Commitment No. 5 ~ *Trusting Source - Giving Up Control and Surrendering to a Higher Purpose* 43
   ~ Self-Commitment No. 6 ~ *Meditation Practice - A Way to Access the Theta State for Hearing Guidance and Healing the Body* 47
   ~ Self-Commitment No. 7 ~ *Provide a Supportive Environment - Choosing Things That Support my Body's Recovery* 51
   ~ Self-Commitment No. 8 ~ *Resting, Resting and More Resting* 55
   ~ Self-Commitment No. 9 ~ *No Deadlines or Time Frames* 58
   ~ Self-Commitment No. 10 ~ *Be Present - Live in the NOW. Enjoy Life* - 62
   ~ Reflecting on the Self-Commitments ~ 65

PART IV ~ The Metaphysical Healing Meditations ~
- ~ By Divine Instruction ~ —69
- ~ The Step-by-Step Guide ~ —71
- ~ STEP 1 ~ Getting Into the Theta State and Connecting to a Higher Power —75
- ~ STEP 2 ~ How to Do a Body Scan and Notice Where Issues Are —80
- ~ STEP 3 ~ How to Apply the Healing Blue Light —85
- ~ STEP 4 ~ How to Listen to and Decipher the Messages Your Body is Revealing to You —88
- ~ STEP 5 ~ Identifying Your Limiting Belief Systems and Replacing Them —94
- ~ STEP 6 ~ Identifying Ancestral Beliefs, Illnesses and Programs and Clearing Them —100
- ~ STEP 7 ~ How to Communicate With Your DNA and Switch ON/OFF Genetic Markers —106
- ~ STEP 8 ~ Communicating With the Cells in Your Body —115
- ~ STEP 9 ~ Forgiveness Work —119
- ~ Conclusion ~ —128

DISCLAIMER —132

APPENDIX I ~ Bonus Healing Activations ~
- ~ Activating Healing Love and Light ~ —i
- ~ Retrieving/Returning Soul Fragments ~ —ii
- ~ Chakra Balancing and Alignment ~ —v
- ~ Activate Protective Light Shield ~ —x

APPENDIX II ~ Reading Recommendations and References ~
- ~ Reading Recommendations ~ —xv
- ~ References ~ —xvii

ACKNOWLEDGMENTS

ABOUT THE AUTHOR

Preface

~ In the Beginning was the Word ~

"In the beginning was the Word, and the Word was with God, and the Word was God." [1]

I heard this spoken early one morning while I was still sleeping, as if a loud voice in my room were speaking it. I woke up understanding its true meaning having never taken notice of it before. I quickly googled it and sure enough, word-for-word there it was, an actual verse in the Bible.

I'm not in the habit of reading the Bible and the last time I even looked at one was probably during Religious Studies at the Catholic school I attended, none of which I ever paid attention to. Since then, my studies have been esoteric and spiritual in nature, but not Catholic doctrine. So how did it come as perfectly as if I'd *just* read it from the book? You can ask Source as it was directly delivered to my subconscious in the dawning of my awakening, both literally and figuratively—waking up from my sleep and awakening from my sleeping life.

This verse would be the knowledge underpinning ALL healing. It is through the spoken word (or words) that we **ask** for healing to be done in the name of **Source** and it *is* done. The beauty of it all is that we carry this ability to heal simply by connecting with Source and asking in Thy name for the healing to be done, and it *is* done.

---

[1] John, 1:1, King James Version.

Further to this, when researching the Word of God, I found that the original name in Hebrew—Yahweh—translates into Hebrew as Yod-Heh-Vav-Heh (YHVH), the **God Code** within creation. The three letters, YHV (the H repeated), are sequenced in varying order to combine and create the DNA codes—the God Codes—written into the very building blocks of our DNA material. These letters become the original building blocks of the amino acids of our DNA. [2]

We have therefore been spoken into existence along with all life. It is thus the essential basis for ALL healing that begins and ends with **the Word** and is activated within us, returning us to the original *Divine Blueprint* as expressly spoken into us in the beginning.

This is the expressway to healing, through the knowledge that the Source of all healing is within us and that all healing begins with **the Word**, returning us to wellness and wellbeing. It is the Divine Creator's wish for all of us to return to this knowing and to reactivate the wellness God Codes.

---

[2] Hurtak, J. J., The Book of Knowledge: The Keys of Enoch, first published 1 December 1982.

Introduction
~ About the Book ~

The following book is based on my self-healing journey. It's the story of how I was *Divinely Instructed* by Source (God) on how to heal myself—how to awaken my own physician within. Over a seven-month period, I trialled my way to recovery from a mystery illness. I was my own guinea pig throughout this process, relying solely on my communication with Source to direct me. I documented my progress as a way to keep me hopeful and focused every day. It was this process that in the end, revealed itself as a program that I could teach others to use.

I have been waiting for the timing of this book coming out to be right, when human consciousness is expanding enough to grasp this information. It's not going to be for everyone as many will find it confronting, but more of us are **waking up** and wanting to learn all that we can to bring back our **lost knowledge** system. We all deserve to be masters of our own selves and self-healing is one of those ways.

The purpose of this book is to reconnect you with your innate knowledge of how to heal yourself. I will show you how to regain this by accessing your own inner wisdom and rebuilding your personal relationship with your spiritual self and **Source**, because these are the foundations in learning to self-heal. We are working with the spiritual extension of yourself; the greater aspect of you, which resides in the ethers, across the veil, waiting to be accessed. That part of you has a direct line to **Source** and, in self-healing, we need not bother with anyone or anything else when we can go directly to the source, because Source is where all healing takes place.

Before I proceed with the book, I want to thank you for choosing to be here. The knowledge was a gift to me and will now be a gift to you. I won't be the first or last to write about metaphysical healing, but I have my own voice to add to the resource library of information that can be drawn on by anyone who wishes to learn. I like to see myself as a transmitter of divine knowledge and my voice may just be the one someone tunes into on the radio waves of transmission. If it resonates with you, then I'm happy. If not, then that's okay to leave it be and go back to what you were doing. Whatever happens, my hope is that you enjoy reading this and maybe even learn something and, if that is the case, I hope you will go on to share it with others.

The world needs this knowledge because we, as a collective human race, are destined for great things. We are truly on the brink of being amazing again, so I hope you will join me on the leading edge of that.

~ Self-Healing Is the New Paradigm ~

The Time is NOW?
How do you know when it's the right time to share this kind of metaphysical knowledge or information? How do you know how it will be received? Will it be celebrated or dissed?

The idea of writing a book about my own self-healing process and teaching others only dawned on me very late in 2020 whilst everyone was in fear of the global virus pandemic. I had originally created it to be a participatory program back in 2019, when I was recovering from my own illness (discussed in Part II). It was to be a series of meditations called *The Metaphysical Healing Meditations*, but it didn't seem as though people were ready for such knowledge yet. In fact, people were sceptical and uncertain. There was interest, but I watched them one-by-one pull out, unable or unwilling to commit to participating in it. In the end, I shelved the whole program, disappointed that something so revolutionary would not be desired. I mean, why on earth wouldn't anyone want to learn how to heal themselves?

You never know what the outcome will be when venturing out into this territory. We often dismiss the existence of anything other than the physical reality we can touch and feel, and yet many of us do believe in something greater than ourselves—a *being of greatness* referred to as **God**—that we are somehow connected to. But for most of us, **He** remains a distant figure, unrelatable to ourselves except through a third-party medium, such as a church representative.

In general, though, the relationship is fraught with contradictory feelings of love/fear, reward/punishment, acceptance/condemnation, and so forth. Believers say, "He loves you. He resides within you," but they never tell you how this relationship actually works. It's like an internal push-pull match of, "He's judging me, but he must love me because he's inside me, right?" No wonder we have a very conflicting relationship with our own spiritual selves. It's all so elusive and confusing, and yet we simply accept it as **faith** because to question it means we are being blasphemous. You simply do not question God or his representatives; that is, until you step back from it all and do the investigating for yourself.

However, to do the research takes time and years of reading, questioning, diving in and surfacing back up to find your way to a contented understanding of the existence of something greater that is not abstract but is entirely relatable. Rather than spirituality being external to us, it resides within us as we discover that, in fact, we are not just *in the likeness of God* but that we are *God Essence*, manifested here on the Earth plane in physical form. This was my greatest revelation.

In discovering this, I found that it was men who created the doctrines, regulations and rules, using God's name to keep us fearful and unquestioning. It is men who created judgment without any God being involved. After years of researching, I developed a deeper, more connected resonance and relationship with **Source**. *He* was no longer male-personified, judgmental, fearful and punishing, but rather loving, compassionate and forever our greatest fan, wanting us to enjoy life whilst learning to be the very best versions of ourselves.

The good news is we are at a collective turning point. More people are waking up to the realities of what they've been conditioned to believe: that their beliefs have been fabricated out of mistruths and misrepresentations of the truth, designed to keep them uninformed, little and disconnected, and separated from the larger part of themselves—their spiritual self. That to me has been the biggest crime of our historical times: denying us access to the knowledge that we innately carry within us.

Historically, documented in numerous books, those responsible for separating us from God through religious doctrines systematically destroyed our ancestors' wisdom. They punished, tortured and executed them for **knowing**, then forcefully imposed a new controlled system of spirituality that was more political and economic in essence than spiritual[3]. We have a right to reclaim our inner knowing. We have the right to discover this for ourselves and forge out of it our own connections with God and the universal essence we carry, because it is us—we are that.

As with all things, however, in this world of **free will** (a Law of this Earth plane) you get to choose what path you take. You get to choose what works for you and live your life according to that, but your free will ends with you. Once you impose onto another then you are taking away *their* free will. That is where the problems are in this world in its current state: everything is being imposed upon you, from your spirituality to your time, and everything is controlled on a linear timeline requiring you to fit in. Obviously, there needs to be some guidelines to govern a society, but once those governing begin erasing or removing the free will of the people, we move away from the so-called democratic societies that are supposed to represent the free world (those that promote free thought, free speech, the freedom to choose) and we fall further away from accessing the very thing we need to keep us existing harmoniously: independence of mind, body and spirit.

The Medical System, aka The Old Paradigm

In my opinion, our current medical system—as advanced as it may appear to be—is stagnating. Considering the technological advancements we have had in the last 20 years, we're not really seeing this translated into medical advancements, not from lack of innovative human discoveries but because they are being controlled. The entire medical system is controlled by pharmaceutical companies, who are in control of the so-called "wellness" system; doctors are controlled by the pharmaceutical companies, and they are paid to prescribe what the "Big Pharmas" (jargon for pharmaceutical companies) order them to promote.

Everything is being treated with a pill these days while our appointment time is reduced, limiting investigation into our illness. We neither get an understanding of our illness nor how

---
[3] Clow, Barbara Hand, *Awakening the Planetary Mind*, first published 21 September 2011.

it may have occurred. There is no time to discuss the prevention of the illness, only a treatment of it. Very rarely are we given a wellness program, or a referral/recommendation to alternative therapies for assistance. Most often we leave the doctor's office less informed than when we went in. We are often simply given a prescription and we accept it, never daring to question or ask, though praising the authority for their wisdom and knowledge, all the while making ourselves more unwell and never actually getting better. Perhaps our version of *better* is just getting lower on the benchmark as society normalises the pill-popping regime.

I will say this: popping pills is never normal. Taking chemicals to make us well is counterintuitive, but for many, that is their belief. In my opinion, I feel as though we are chemically overloading our bodies, making it harder for them to cope. We may even be poisoning them instead of healing them. I also believe that many practitioners are willing to go along with the idea that pharmaceuticals are the answer to everything, and this has led to the stagnation of the medical system. Instead of the wellness of patients being the optimum focus and goal, the medical profession seems to prefer saving time and making more money. In my experience, fast Band-Aid treatments are all too common practice now for physical and mental health, often leading to endless cycles of trialling treatments but never quite curing anything. Sometimes, you really are the guinea pig. It's food for thought, anyway.

I'm not going to spend too much time focusing on pharmaceuticals being the suppliers, doctors being the dealers, and us being the addicts, but I am hoping, if nothing else, that your curiosity has been piqued and you may consider investigating the system a little more.

*NOTE: It is totally up to you if you wish to investigate the pharmaceutical companies for yourself. However, if you do not wish to acknowledge this and wish to remain connected with your medical protocols because you trust they are in your best interest, then it is entirely your choice to do so. It will not interfere with the self-healing program. Many clients and participants in my courses have chosen to remain aligned with the

medical system and their prescribed medications. Others have opted to use alternative treatments that they align with.

Pause here for a moment and consider what we are unknowingly taking into our system on a daily basis just from our environment:
- the air
- the water
- the earth
- the animals we eat
- the food we buy.

Everything—unless certified organic or certified non-genetically modified (non-GMO)—*is* contaminated and polluted with chemicals and radiation. This is what we are ingesting, which over the years (even intergenerationally) has built up in our systems and is making us unwell. So, adding chemicals into our already toxic body systems in the form of pills, may not be the most helpful way we can support our bodies.

I have experienced this medical/pharmaceutical partnership myself and witnessed it first-hand when I worked as part of stakeholders' teams for patients and clients suffering from mental health. I also observed my mother's rheumatoid arthritis and cancer treatments over a 20-year period and how she suffered, not just from the illnesses but from the many side effects eventuating from her multiple medication protocols. Unfortunately, her body simply couldn't recover enough to be well, continually trying to heal the condition caused by the medications for the previous condition. This was a sentence that she endured graciously, never once questioning, only surrendering fully to a system that treated her like a guinea pig. Yet it was what she chose for herself, and she was committed to that decision. Perhaps her journey has inspired me to pursue self-healing as a gentler tool.

I still like to believe that many medical practitioners are well-intentioned and maintain some integrity. Sadly, there are very few *old school* doctors still in existence. The ones that thoroughly check you out and ask you investigative questions. The ones that still have higher intentions in relation to your wellbeing. I prefer these doctors when looking for good information. I like to be well informed as it helps me when I'm doing my healing work and gives me a starting point to work with.

But I believe everything has its place. If we were in an accident, we'd want immediate emergency medical treatment. Emergency crews are incredible, and they do amazing work saving lives. It's the long-term treatments for illnesses requiring extensive medical intervention that I am concerned about. It's here that I want you to take control of your own health, valuing your body's wellness, and implement your own **healing** in order to achieve this goal.

What I am noticing is a growing trend away from medical interventions and a desire for more alternative, complementary methods of achieving healing and wellness. We are doing our homework and researching alternative options for treatments that support or enhance our body's natural immunity and self-healing. We want to be well informed in order to make more self-aligned decisions. We all want the freedom to choose what's right for us. We want autonomy over our healing and to have some say in our own medical or therapeutic treatments.

Even if you still would like to continue being a part of the medical system (no judgement here), then I want you to be aware of what else you can do to promote your own healing. You are not powerless. In fact, you are very powerful and have the capacity to do amazing things. You just need to know how.

The New Paradigm—Self-Healing
I want to introduce to you the very thing I wish to discuss in this book: your innate ability to **heal** yourself, emotionally, mentally and physically. You, my dear friends, have the power to do this and so much more. You don't need to be a genius to learn this technique. I have done the hard part of learning it *By Divine Instruction* directly from Source, then pulling it all together to deliver it in an easy-to-understand format.

The goal is for you to develop confidence in working on yourself so you will be able to work on your own body. Like anything, it takes time, so you need to learn the theory first, the application of it second and then practice, practice, practice 'til you perfect it. Then perhaps one day, you will be so confident in your abilities that you'll choose to be your own intuitive physician and treat yourself like I did and still do.

Before I learned how to self-heal or understand how illnesses were linked to, or brought on by, my emotional distress and inner disharmony, I (like everyone else) relied on antibiotics and antidepressants. Yet I've never become dependent on any interventions, often doing whatever I could to recover myself. I've found even taking painkillers or anti-inflammatories haven't agreed with me, usually making me nauseous, so I've limited my use of these over-the-counter drugs. But like others, when I was sick, I took a pill or went to a doctor to get a prescription 'til I questioned what I was doing and learned better.

Once I became more aware, whenever I was sick, I would work on improving not just my health, but my environment, relationships, life in general. I intuitively believed that my health was the sum of my whole world—emotional, mental and physical—and that each played an integral part in my wellbeing. Self-awareness was therefore the most important aspect of learning to be my own healer. You have to know yourself in order to understand when your body is out of alignment, why it's out, and how to bring it back into alignment. Thus, becoming attuned to your mental and emotional systems assists immensely in learning to self-heal.

Many of us are not even aware that our body is a living organism that listens and responds to what's going on in our lives. We don't even take the time to look at what triggers the unwellness in our system. Often, we just look at the symptoms and focus on that, then act from there. If only we understood *why* our body was behaving a certain way and then **acted** from there, we'd not only be able to address the symptoms but also the cause. However, in all honesty, we are often reluctant to change what we're doing in order to help ourselves because we fear change itself.

These days, I'm more hesitant to accept chemical treatments than I may have been in the past prior to learning how to work *with* my body and my mind, especially when faced with long-term medical or chemical interventions. I try to find an alternative way that I can use alongside medical intervention if I must, but on its own, preferably. I like having the power to choose and say, "Thank you for your information. I feel informed enough to say *no* to that treatment," and then go on my way to activate my self-healing protocol.

I had the perfect opportunity to test this out with the mystery illness, which I'll be discussing in Part II. It was the catalyst for my greatest learning: that of self-healing and how powerful our minds are as a tool for this. It would also be the driving force behind letting go of the old paradigm of **helping** people and shifting to **healing** people in a more spiritual and metaphysical way—a total shift in paradigm.

Now, I feel like "illness" is no longer something to be afraid of. I never feel afraid of catching colds, flus, or other contagious/infectious diseases because I know that my body is in alignment. I feel so in charge of my body that I never seem to attract these undesirable things into my life anymore. If I have felt under the weather, I know immediately something needs addressing and I get to work on it while resting. Within twenty-four hours, whatever began showing up has left my body, never getting a chance to settle in and take over. This is the power of self-healing.

That is why I believe self-healing *is* a new paradigm. We are not just reducing our reliance on the medical system and medications but shifting our mindset away from the old **fear** model of relating to illness, moving towards a positive, self-empowered model of healing. It's also freeing us up from our dependence on external services because we can do some of the work ourselves. There are so many benefits to self-healing, such as:

- saving time and money on doctors' visits or hospital stays
- less medications
- less time missing work

- more time with family
- more time enjoying life
- feeling empowered and in charge.

And that's just to name a few. It's also about you feeling confident to make decisions pertaining to *your* wellness treatments.

I believe this is the next collective leap in our evolution where we will be able to treat ourselves. We'll no longer be relying on toxic substances to make us feel better but rather, accessing our innate wisdom and knowledge to heal ourselves and remain well. This book is therefore not just about making you feel good, but is designed to inform, teach, and guide you through the transition from **old paradigm** medical systems to **new paradigm** self-healing systems.

So, are you ready to begin healing yourself today? Because self-healing really *is* the **new paradigm**!

Part I
~ About Me ~

~ Who Am I? ~

Very briefly, because my life could fill volumes, I'd like to introduce myself to you.

I am Ann Basili and I was born in Perth, Western Australia in 1970 to Egyptian parents who migrated to Australia in 1969. Born in between worlds—Egyptian and Australian—was not easy. Like most first generation Aussies, I wanted to fit in with Australian culture whilst my parents wanted to pass on their traditional culture to keep their cultural heritage alive. So, there was always a lot of tension for me as an Egyptian/Australian daughter.

Their expectations for me were huge from the time I was born, and being a female in a liberated country with very strict, often oppressive, parents was even harder. As I got older, we clashed over pretty much everything. We fought constantly due to the very restrictive and confined rules. My rebellion against their tradition or culture wasn't all about being a female in a liberated country though; it was mostly to do with the fact I was the victim of family violence.

My father was an extremely controlling and physically abusive man, often wielding his power with great physical force. This began when I was a very small child and continued 'til I left home at around 16 years of age. My mother was also emotionally unavailable and unable to show me love. She was always so controlling and highly critical, criticising me at every opportunity. She put me down constantly and never offered praise or kindness. She was often cruel with her words and found ways to isolate or alienate me. My childhood, therefore, was a lonely one, where I sat very obviously on the outside. Whilst my father was physically abusive, my mother was psychologically abusive. As a result, I learned to wear heavy armour right up into my early forties.

My father left my mother when I was about 17 and moved to the

Eastern states of Australia. To be honest, this was a very happy time for me, and I only ever connected with him a handful of times after that. My mother and I sadly never really found our place or peace together (not from my lack of trying) until the week before she passed away. She died following many years of suffering, as I mentioned in the last chapter. I felt both great grief and relief: grief because I would never **feel loved** by her, and relief because I could exhale for the very first time. I finally felt safe to take off my armour and to tend to the deep wounds and trauma that lay beneath.

This would take a lot of dedicated inner work and self-healing. Forgiveness would come eventually for my parents, but it would take me many years, and I'd become very sick before I'd finally deal with the deep wounding and let go of all the suffering that had robbed me of my life. My inherited culture equated with lots of anger, physical abuse and trauma, and very little to do with love and affection. As a result, disconnecting from my birth family was paramount if I wanted to survive.

I spent most of my life alone navigating the world around me as best as I could, without any support or a solid loving platform to launch out from. Life was very difficult for me, suffering ongoing bouts of crippling depression and anxiety, but I wasn't officially diagnosed until I was 25, following the birth of my daughter. From there, I would embark on a very challenging solo mothering venture. I would spend 18 years hanging onto the edge of the cliff of survival and, at times, find myself at the very bottom of the abyss, isolated and alone. Regardless, I never gave up on my determination to be the very best mother I could be—the mother I wished I'd had. I was so hard on myself and afraid of failing constantly. It was tough going because my world was always informed by my trauma.

Unfortunately, I would never really experience a truly loving relationship with anyone else in my life. All relationships equated to suffering and pain. Not knowing what it's like to be truly loved by my parents made it incredibly difficult to know what love is and how to recognise it. Instead, I was constantly reaching for things that were familiar to me, repeating patterns with each relationship until I woke up one day and said, "I've had enough! It's time to let go of all this shit!" and learned to love myself.

The giving of love I thought would be the most challenging but in fact, it was the easiest. Through my challenging "indigo child" daughter, I learned about love, not any love but **unconditional love**. Learning to love myself in the absence of the experience of love was so much harder. It was missing from my soul-learning on Earth. Receiving love was also a whole other issue because I was so unable to let it in, never feeling deserving or worthy of it. It wasn't until I learned about loving myself that I understood that in order to be loved you had to be love. I had to love myself first.

What's the relevance of sharing this with you, you may ask? Well, **love** and **forgiveness** are two of the most important elements in self-healing. You'll learn more about this as you work through the book.

Social Conscience
I believe I was born **awake**—awake to the world's corruptions and injustices. As far back as I can remember, I always had a strong social conscience, taking notice of things that did not quite appear fair or just, even as a small child. I believe my childhood experience awakened my ability to recognise situations that were unjust, such as discrimination and violence against women, the abuse of children, racism against indigenous people (of all nations) and those of African descent, socio-economic inequality, and more.

My parents, although coming from a Christian background, could often be intolerant of others' differences and yet, they could be quite generous in other ways—mainly giving to 'the poor'. So, I do not feel I inherited my social conscience from them or from Christianity, although I do feel my generosity and giving of spirit was a Christian value.

Later on in life, I would try to make sense out of my social awareness by doing a Sociology degree. Sociology took all my intuitive understandings and gave me a framework to intellectually analyse our social systems and critique them. I loved it. However, it also depressed me seeing how much of our modern systems had underlying issues that perpetuated injustices rather than alleviate them. Once the lid was lifted, I saw injustices, discrimination and corruption everywhere. I therefore became a passionate advocate, protesting on a variety of causes, fighting for equality, justice and freedom. I was quite the social warrior.

I toned down my protesting activities once my daughter was born. By the time she was ready for school, I was prepared to channel my social conscience back into the employment world. But I wanted to align with the direction I was moving in, away from a theoretical, academic way of assisting people, and towards a more practical, hands-on approach. I would morph again, ten years later, from a practical Social Work career to a spiritually aligned healing practice.

Qualifications
Despite my personal history, I still managed to create a successful life for myself. I qualified professionally with two University degrees: a combined Bachelor of Sociology and Anthropology (1991-1994) and a Bachelor of Social Work (2000-2002), the first two years of which were accredited due to my previous degree.

Sociology and Anthropology enabled me to gain a deep, expansive understanding of how cultures evolved: from tribal beginnings connected to each other, the Earth and the heavens, to current modern societies with more emphasis on separation from each other, and a disconnect from the Earth and the heavens. It was an intricate critical assessment and scrutinisation of how our societies are created and how we are conditioned to live in them. It enhanced my social consciousness and social awareness and gave me the ability to be very insightful and socially critical. I therefore have a very good eye for the hidden details, and a great ear for the hidden narratives.

Social work, on the other hand, took me deeper into understanding the psyche and traumas of humans. I initially set out to do a Psychology degree but, within a year, I found it was so detached and diminishing of the human experience that it repelled me. Social work, on the other hand, seemed to humanise individuals more, empathising with the human experience and seeing them as a result of the systems they grew up in. I found it more appealing with greater diversity in professional opportunities.

Social Work would take me on a comprehensive career journey working in many areas: mental health, welfare, homelessness, domestic violence, crisis, youth suicide, youth work, therapeutic and clinical counselling, and research. I worked in not-for-profit and non-government agencies, as well as government-funded organisations and hospitals, giving me an insightful perspective on how our systems operate.

In my opinion and experience, these assistance and welfare organisations were often toxic cultures/systems which were designed to help but not heal. The mental health system was referred to as a **revolving door** because it was like an endless cycle of people entering in crisis, treated with medications, exiting with little in the way of support networks in place, and eventually returning to the health system to begin the process over again. Some organisations were better at offering help and keeping people out of this system but often, once reliant on these systems, it was very hard to truly break free and become autonomous. Sadly, after ten years of witnessing these flawed health and welfare systems, I was disappointed and burnt out.

After completing these degrees, I invested many years continuing my professional development, often spending weekends attending courses in order to gain extra accreditation or certification in compatible therapeutic models. Over the years, I would expand that training to include alternative health and spiritual healing models of therapy when I felt my clients would be better served with more targeted knowledge. Thus, I became certified in Female Sexuality Education and Healing, ThetaHealing®, and Quantum Healing Hypnosis Technique® (QHHT®). After leaving my Social Work career, I set up my first private counselling practice specialising in depression and anxiety, relationships, sex/intimacy counselling and working with women suffering from sexual trauma.

ThetaHealing®[4] was the first formal training I'd had in an alternative healing modality. It's where my psychic skills were fine-tuned. This modality is all about healing by using your third eye to visualise and connect with Source. This would be the beginning of my true understanding of Divine connection and how Source is the portal to all healing. It was the foundation for my spiritual evolution and learning to use my healing and psychic abilities. I would learn and grow exponentially from this training, and I know that without it, I wouldn't have been able to advance my own abilities and morph them into how I work today.

By 2017, I was offering this as a healing modality for clients. Over time, I became less reliant on ThetaHealing® and more trusting in my own abilities, allowing them to evolve organically using my direct connection to Source. This would eventually lead me to being divinely taught the *Metaphysical Healing Meditations (MHMs)*, but I owe my initial foray into healing to the ThetaHealing® training.

I began transitioning away from mainstream counselling and offering more healing and spiritually focused services. Though I'd begun offering ThetaHealing®, I felt there was something else I needed, so in 2019, after recovering from my mystery illness and having just created the *MHMs*, I decided to train as a Quantum Healing Hypnosis Technique® practitioner (QHHT®), developed by the late Dolores Cannon[5]. Within a year, I'd completed my internship and my level 1 and level 2 certifications. I found this technique built on my professional, therapeutic and spiritual attributes and it was an awesome healing tool for clients still wanting guidance from a practitioner. It was the missing piece to my professional work.

QHHT® is a comprehensive way for people to heal on all levels—mentally, emotionally and physically, from the past right up to the

---

[4] Stibal, Vianna, https://www.thetahealing.com, accessed September 2023
[5] https://www.dolorescannon.com

present and into the future. This type of healing made complete sense to me. I found it to be the perfect bridge for people who hadn't yet decided they wanted to learn to **self-heal** but wanted to venture into the alternative world of "healing". They would still heal themselves but with the guidance of a practitioner. After this experience, it was possible that they would feel more confident to step across the threshold into the self-healing paradigm and be open to trying something like the *MHMs*.

~ Spiritual and Healing Evolution ~

Spiritual Beginnings
In order to understand how I connected and received Divine Instruction from Source, it helps to have some background into my upbringing, which fostered my openness to the spiritual realms. In hindsight, I see how it was like a training ground, preparing me to reach beyond the limitations of the physical realms. All the spiritual guidance and instruction from my mother was subconsciously preparing me to open up and receive this *Divine Instruction*. It was not planned, nor was it obvious to anyone that this is what was happening. It only occurred to me over the last few years and I'm able to draw on all the training I had that now resides within me. In that way, I was able to connect and receive the **divine guidance** I required to heal my body and myself.

In my world, the spiritual realms overlapped with the physical realms and being psychic was just an extension of who I was. I began learning about the spiritual realms early in my childhood. My mother was very spiritually connected and open with her spiritual awareness and knowledge. From early on, she communicated with me about the paranormal, the spiritual and metaphysical. I learned to meditate at around the age of eight and was introduced to the concept of reincarnation, past lives and the afterlife; how souls become earth bound and could possess humans. She spoke of and practiced astral travelling/projection and taught me more fun occult aspects like tarot reading, palmistry and astrology. My mother encouraged my psychic gifts but always warned against using them for monetary or commercial gain. It was only through this spiritual teaching and sharing that I found some connection with my mother. My spiritual awareness is therefore her legacy; her gift to me.

At the age of two, I recalled detailed past life experiences and could naturally astral travel. I could observe and report in great detail on places I'd never seen or been to before. I could sense ghosts but didn't wish to see them. I could sense what people were going to say before they said it (telepathic) and feel what they were feeling (empathic). Meditation, however, would probably become the most useful out of all my spiritual experiences. Through learning meditation, I was able to activate my **third eye**, which is the portal to the higher dimensional realms. It is connected to the pineal gland, which is referred to as "the seat of the soul"[6]. Once you learn to activate this, you can access spiritual, metaphysical and quantum realms. This is where you connect to Source and where healing takes place.

When I was 15, I learned Transcendental Meditation, which is a meditation technique that could bring you into the deeper states of relaxation and consciousness. It was during this period that I saw and connected with my first spiritual **guide**. He was an elderly sage, wearing a loincloth sitting in the lotus position next to me. We did not communicate but I felt a deep sense of comfort knowing he was there beside me. I would go on to have many different guides throughout my life. Perhaps my most influential guide was a Native American **medicine woman** of the Blackfoot people. She has, in many ways integrated with me by **soul merging**, which is the best way to describe it, sharing many metaphysical and cosmic secrets. Alongside my spiritual healing training, she has been instrumental in assisting me to grow and heal myself, so that I may become the best healer I can be.

Spiritual Influences and Influencers
Having grown up Christian but always questioning its teachings and ritual practices, I began researching all major religions. As part of my degree in Sociology and Anthropology, I spent a year studying Theology and how and why religions were created. I found Hinduism and Buddhism appealing and took some of their teachings, like reincarnation, mindfulness and respecting all life forms, and added them into my spiritual belief system.

Another major area of my investigation, which had a more feminist approach, was in relation to how women were mainly

---
[6] As described by Rene' Descartes.

seen as subordinate to men in the eyes of the Church, putting Mary Magdalene front and centre in my inquiry. My investigation led me to discover that, in fact, She was a major player in Jesus's closest network and was an Apostle of the highest order. Mary was also an incredible healer, working alongside Jesus, and she was considered a close companion to him, something the Church has denied. They instated a "whore" narrative to maintain the view that women are not worthy of equality in the eyes of God, unless you are Jesus's mother, Mary.

Mary Magdalene has been a major spiritual influence and influencer in my life. She has continued to inspire me and help me to embody the fullness of God, just as She did. Her true story revealed in the Dead Sea scrolls, the Nag Hammadi library, and historical and spiritual books, has opened my eyes to the more controversial aspects of Christianity, the Church as we know it today, and the life of Jesus. I have continued this research up to today, finding much groundbreaking information that turns the whole bible story around **Her** on its head (see Appendix II).

Another wonderful spiritual influencer for me was Sai Baba, an Indian Guru. I was introduced to His teachings when I was going through a tough period in my life as a single mother. Although I'd been actively working on myself psychologically, I was still not quite finding that "X" factor that would really help me heal. I wanted a non-judgmental, non-condemning antidote to the Christian tradition I'd grown up in. I longed for loving ways to understand my life and Sai Baba offered that to me.

I never travelled to India, nor did I ever meet Sai Baba, but I always felt a connection to him from the moment I started studying his teachings. He was warm, loving, kind, sweet, generous, and accepting. He was like the mother and father I never had. In fact, his name literally translates to "Mother/Father of ALL". I cried a lot because all the teachings were about loving yourself, and that:
- no matter who you are, you are worthy and loveable
- you are perfect as you are
- God loves you despite what you have done or not done

- there is unconditional love to be had, even if you can't access it from those in your life
- it is there for you through God
- there is so much worthiness in this life.

I learned that I am of God and connected to God, not separate from God. I was that. I *am* that.

Sai Baba's teachings reached into my heart and soul. Knowing that someone loved me for who I was despite all my flaws and damage was the real wonder. I felt truly valued and worthy. He helped to reignite my sense of self, my spiritual self, which I allowed to be present with me always from then on. I began witnessing the little miracles in life, keeping me comforted and in full faith.

Unexplainable Influences

From an early age, I became fascinated by the phenomena of Crop Circles, Unidentified Flying Objects (UFOs) and Aliens/Extra Dimensionals (EDs). Over the years, my intrigue has led me to understand how intrinsically linked spirituality is with these phenomena. Spiritual growth means accessing higher dimensional frequencies. As EDs exist in these higher dimensional realms and frequencies, we come closer to connecting with them, thereby understanding more about ourselves and our place in the Universe.

Dolores Cannon's material on UFOs and EDs contributed much to my understanding due to her candid openness on the subject. But we are only beginning to open up to the possibility of other species existing within our galaxy. I feel that we are on the precipice of something huge for our own kind. I believe that through healing ourselves collectively and becoming more unified, the possibilities of connecting to the higher dimensions with our extraterrestrial brothers and sisters may become a reality. Amazing times ahead.

Spiritual Awakening

The magic of my life began revealing itself to me in 2015. It was the beginning of my spiritual awakening. This process is often preceded by the **Dark Night of the Soul**, considered a time where one reaches the depths of despair and enters the meaninglessness of life. It is traumatic and filled with many feelings, including fear, grief, despair, aloneness, abandonment, rejection, and so on. All of your deepest, darkest aspects are forced to the surface to be contended with—a reckoning of the self. It can trigger suicidal ideations if no inner self-worth or resilience can be found in the darkness. It consists of reviewing all your hurts/traumas/wounds and eventually, with grace, healing and releasing of all of them, including limiting belief systems and conditioning. It is also characterised by the death of the **ego self**: the death of your identity, letting it go so you are essentially left as nothing—a complete blank slate. Nothing exists from the former self, and nothing is created yet of the new self. One exists in a void.

It can take some years before the creating of the new self begins. But the time between destruction and (re)creation *is* the key to birthing the most aligned version of your true self, because a lot of thought and contemplation happens during this state. When one befriends the darkness and surrenders, it can be a time of much-needed respite and quietness for the new self to be born. This is a sacred time and one that should be revered rather than seen as a mental condition or breakdown. The true self needs to emerge in its own timing.

It is also the birthing of a more fully developed spiritual or higher sense of self. The one that recognises the **divine** connection to the Universe, to God, and to ALL things. It is not linked to a religion or ideology. It is pure Source connection. It is from this state that an expansion of consciousness takes place and suddenly you are no longer this small, disconnected, solo being, but a huge, interconnected, **divine soul** being of such tremendous power.

I personally experienced all this turmoil. It was a harrowing experience, like being spun vigorously in a washing machine and then spat out into a river, watching myself float away downstream. It was unbearable and something I thought I'd never survive. But I not only survived, I thrived. I was shaken out of my old self and reawakened in a brand new state to begin over. My spiritual awakening was not a kind experience—it was cruel and torturous—

but being reborn is not an easy or simple procedure, and it requires much time and tolerance. When you cannot see the light, it is frightening, but the light always comes, starting tiny and growing 'til it surrounds you. That is the metamorphic experience Ascended Masters speak of. It is not for the faint-hearted.

I feel in order to heal and ascend to reach higher dimensions, we need to activate this awakening state for ourselves. If only we didn't have to reach the depths of despair to do so. But from my own experience and having spent years observing and working closely with other humans, I conclude that it may be the *only* way humans learn and grow. It is therefore from this place, that we are truly able to let go of the past fully and finally to embrace our present. This will be the birthing of the **New Human** (the higher dimensional human), and when we arrive, we will reclaim our place on Earth and unite all beings together as was the original divine plan.

By the time I landed back into myself and was thriving in my new self, I felt truly connected and whole for the very first time. I felt like I'd made a quantum leap into another dimension. I was on fire—a fire of spiritual light. My healing abilities had lain dormant during my transitional period but were now fully activated. My intuition was showing me and teaching me how to connect to my world differently, to **sense** my world and **feel** my world using my awakened sixth sense abilities, rather than my five 3D senses. I felt like I'd had a major makeover from the inside out and, more importantly, the timing of it all was crucial.

I was right on track and on time to help with a global spiritual movement that was initiated by the ending of the Mayan calendar in 2012. This was the ending of a major cycle, a Great Age, and the transition from the Age of Pisces to the Age of Aquarius.

Awakening and the New Earth

The global transition we are about to go through is referred to as The Awakening or the **New Earth**[7] that coincides with the dawning of the Age of Aquarius[8]. It's going to cause a major rift and fracture

---

7 Cannon, Dolores, The Three Waves of Volunteers and the New Earth, first published 1 June 2011.
8 Clow, Barbara Hand, Revelations of the Aquarian Age, published 13 February 2018.

in society. The old paradigm is timing out, whilst a new paradigm is being launched. This is the turning point, and tipping point, for society as the world awakens to a spiritual dawn after a long dark slumber.

It is not going to be an easy transition because many institutions will begin to break down, including the Church, the governments, and the medical systems. There will be great resistance from these systems, as well as from individuals who try to push back, refusing to accept that change is coming. But it *will* happen and many of us, including myself, are already actively participating and assisting others through this transition. Collectively, it is all about healing— healing the self, healing the Earth, and healing our relationships with each other. This is how *we* transition to the New Earth.

The Awakening movement has grown exponentially. We have literally accelerated in our spiritual learning and are changing the face of this planet in record numbers across the globe. Spirituality is no longer about religion; it's about personal spirituality and your sovereign connection directly with God. We are transitioning from the base-line physical, mundane world to the heart-line spiritual/metaphysical one. The world is readying itself for a great shift in consciousness and therefore requires more liberating, expansive and spiritually connected ways for things to be done, including healing our minds, bodies and spirits.

Being on the leading edge of this global movement, we are raising the consciousness of humanity through our healing work. The *MHMs* are a part of this expansion program. I'm so very excited to showcase my learning and my understanding of living immersed in the spiritual world and how you can use that knowledge to self-heal, not just emotionally, but physically as well.

Are you ready to make the shift and embrace your spiritual awakening through self-healing?

Part II

~ The Illness ~

~ The Mystery Illness ~

I have always trusted my body to know what it needs to get well. I just didn't know in the early days why I knew this or how the body did it, let alone know how to assist the process of healing it. Over the years, I've had several incidents that should have required hospitalisation, medical or chemical intervention, or even surgery that I had declined, not due to deep knowledge of my body but rather, due to a **feeling** guiding me not to go through with it. I intuitively knew that if I rested long enough, eventually my body would recover.

For the couple of minor surgeries I've had in my lifetime (the removal of my appendix at eight-years-old and gallbladder at 47), I have mostly looked after myself and healed myself. I do accept that there is a time when the removal of toxic/septic elements in my body are essential to my recovery, especially if they are prone to cause harm to the rest of my body. Yet, I always remain vigilant and informed, and proceed on my own terms wherever possible. That's not to say I've never taken medical treatments in the past, because I have.

In the instances where I'd damaged ligaments or broken bones, I would access a little extra assistance. I'd have it checked properly and, if necessary, put in a cast. If I required physiotherapy, I would attend a couple of sessions, learn the exercises, and then spend the rest of the time applying the techniques and caring for myself. When I knew what the issue was, I would meditate on that area and let my body heal.

The Minor Tests
When I was 17, not long after I graduated from High School, I contracted glandular fever, which lasted nearly a whole year. I was bedridden a lot of the time but, when I wasn't lying in bed, I was out pushing my own limits, inevitably delaying the healing process. I was too young to understand the implications of my ignorance

of 'self-care', but I healed eventually without too much medical support.

At the age of 27, I got dengue fever in a remote island village off the coast of Thailand. I lay delirious in a tiny hut, unconscious for nearly a week before someone found me and sent me to a remote hospital. There was no running water, no food, no medicine, and no doctors; just an attendant checking my saline drip. They graciously kept me there for two days, then discharged me because they didn't have the resources to help me.

With all my courage, a raging fever and a handful of painkillers, I managed to travel for two days to get to the mainland, where I was diagnosed over the phone by a doctor in Canberra who said to me, "Do not move, or fly, or go anywhere for two weeks. It's critical as you are at risk of haemorrhaging. If this occurs, you will die." So, I stayed put in a cheap villa for two weeks, sleeping.

I began losing the sight in my left eye and my hair started falling out. I was also very jaundiced due to the high toxins in my system which were overloading my liver. After two weeks of literally doing nothing, I recovered enough to fly out and return to Bali, where I was living at the time. Once there, the locals brought a great traditional healer to me, who helped remove the toxins from my body and alleviate my body's distress through a series of intense, deep tissue, full body massages. I remained in Bali for three months before returning home to Australia.

In total, it took me two years to recover from the dengue, but I did so without medical intervention, mostly because there wasn't any, and I had no choice but to heal. I give thanks and gratitude to the carers in that tiny remote Thai village hospital, and to the angels—Earth and spiritual ones—who held me safe as best they could. I would've died in that village on my own if not for them. That's why I knew it was not my time to pass over yet and that I was definitely being **divinely** supported.

The Major Test

In 2019, when I was 48, I experienced a major health challenge. This would be the first *real* healing journey test that I would be exposed to. It would require me to use all aspects of my spiritual knowledge. It would also require great trust and faith in my healing abilities and in my connection with **Source**, because that was the only constant that I knew I had. I would become my own science experiment with me being my own guinea pig. I had little to no knowledge of what the issue was or what the potential outcome could or would be.

In May of that year, I got the flu. There was nothing extraordinary about it, nor was it unlike any flu I'd had in the past. My body ached, my head hurt, and I had a sore throat and a congested respiratory system. I spent a couple of weeks resting and let my body's immunity do its thing naturally. Although I recovered as was expected, I awoke one morning a couple of weeks later to find my elbow was sore, as though I'd banged it against something hard. It was painful to the touch, and I couldn't bend or stretch my arm. This persisted for a few weeks but still I didn't worry too much about it.

Along with experiencing this elbow pain, my left knee suddenly became painful and wouldn't bend easily. I couldn't think what had caused my knee to be in pain without reason. Within 24 hours, I couldn't even walk on that leg. My knee was swollen to the size of a rockmelon, filled with fluid and hot to the touch. I couldn't bend it at all. By this stage, I was starting to query the link between my elbow and my knee. Were they related? And if so, what was the trigger?

I reviewed the weeks leading up to these issues presenting and the only precursor to this strange situation was the flu. I researched my symptoms on the internet to see if there was information relating to my situation, but I couldn't find anything. After a couple of weeks of no relief, I decided to see a doctor just to get some insight into what was happening to me.

As I don't have a family doctor, I requested to see whichever doctor was on duty that day. She ran some tests on me, which came up with a collection of autoimmune-related illnesses or diseases. It was also suggested that the flu I'd had was some kind of virus which triggered these symptoms, but she had no idea what kind of virus it could be or how it linked to the autoimmune diseases. So essentially, the illness was all a great mystery and the treatments she proposed were, therefore, going to be experimental. I said to her, "This treatment doesn't make sense to me as it's going to affect my whole body, making me unwell, rather than just targeting the area of my body that is actually unwell. As it is, I can still function with the rest of my body even if limited. Thank you for your time. I wanted to be informed and you have done that. But I am not going to proceed with your proposal. I'm going to treat myself." But things were going to get worse before getting any better.

I began applying my healing techniques and I was just starting to feel some relief in my left leg when, without warning, the same symptoms began in my right leg. If I thought my left leg was bothersome, this leg was a screamer. I was in absolute agony. My right leg swelled up overnight, becoming excruciating, and I had a fever to go with it. Before I knew it, I was no longer able to use either leg and I became very unwell.

I was in disbelief as to how this—whatever it was—could jump from my elbow to my left knee then into my right knee. There was simply no rhyme or reason. I researched the diagnoses I'd been given by the doctor, but nothing was resonating. This mystery illness had literally appeared without warning, and I had very little to go on. As I stubbornly refused to go down the medical route, I had no choice but to sort it out fast.

So began my in-depth, inward journey of self-discovery and self-healing. I was going to be totally devoted to, and look after, myself. In essence, I was making a commitment (or pledge) that I would find the answer and heal myself. While looking back at what I'd achieved, it wouldn't be 'til after I'd completed my healing journey that I would realise the importance of this aspect of it. I hadn't learnt this; I had intuitively known this. As such, I am going to articulate the commitments that will help you on your own self-healing journey.

Part III

~ Committing to Yourself and Your Body ~

~ Self-Commitments ~

What are Self-Commitments and Why are They Important?

When I embarked on my self-healing journey, I became very disciplined and committed to a series of thoughts and actions to help keep me focused while I healed my body. These I called *Self-Commitments*, which would be the foundations for all self-healing.

I like to think of them in the following way: When you train for a sports event and you want to be in peak condition, you become disciplined and make sure to do all the right things in order to get you to that goal. You eat right, exercise a certain way, get good amounts of sleep, stay away from stressful environments, and so on. You are *committed* to yourself to make sure you've done everything in your power to be in top shape in order to perform optimally in the sports event. With healing, it's the same but our goal is our wellbeing rather than a sports event. We commit to ourselves in the same way though, looking after ourselves to help us reach our goal of wellness.

I identified ten *Self-Commitments* listed below. Read more about each one in the subsequent chapters to understand the importance of each of them and how to apply them.

~ The Ten Self-Commitments ~

No. 1 ~ Commitment to my body—Do I accept and love this body?

No. 2 ~ The Power of a positive mind—Positive thoughts and speech. What you speak about you bring about.

No. 3 ~ Do you believe? Challenging and replacing limiting beliefs.

No. 4 ~ No fear—Releasing any fear of the unknown.

No. 5 ~ Trusting **Source**—Giving up control and surrendering to a higher purpose.

No. 6 ~ Meditation practice—A way to access the Theta state for hearing guidance and healing the body.

No. 7 ~ Provide a supportive environment—Choosing things that support my body's recovery.

No. 8 ~ Resting, resting and more resting.

No. 9 ~ Patience—No deadlines or time frames.

No. 10 ~ Be Present—Live in the **NOW**. Enjoy life.

~ Self-Commitment No. 1 ~
Commitment to My Body
Do I Accept and Love This Body?

The first important element in the healing equation is deciding whether you commit to your body. Are you committed to being *in* it? Are you committed to wanting to align *with* it? Are you committed to *loving* it?

I grew up in the world without being taught how to love my body or appreciate it. My first foray into becoming aware that there was something wrong with my body's physical appearance was at age eight, when my mother took me to the doctor complaining that I was too fat. I didn't even know that I was fat or that it was a thing to be worried about. I recall the doctor commenting, "Yes she's got a spare tyre and could lose some weight," and they promptly put me on a diet. This would end up being the beginning of my lifelong battle with my weight, my self-image and myself. I learned from that day on that my body was not okay and that I had to work against it for it to look acceptable.

The world around me suddenly shifted and I became highly aware of my body's issues—*my* issues. As I grew older, instead of being micromanaged by my mother, I took over the reins and managed myself with much self-loathing and a high degree of self-discipline. Socially, those around me mirrored what my mother's expectations were of me. I learned that these conditions I was being subjected to were necessary for me to be accepted in the world and, ideally, be considered "worthy". But on reflection, with much maturity and self-love, I see a very destructive initiation into the world and how my body was constantly under scrutiny. I see how, very early on, I was conditioned to view my body as the enemy and that I needed to fight it, setting me up to consider my body as a problem.

I'm sure I'm not the only one who grew up this way. I'm certain, in one way or another, you may have grown up with some conditioning that was not about making friends with your body but rather, seeing it as troublesome and something to be loathed. Our media, too, has been promoting this for as long as I can recall—to be thinner, fitter, healthier, prettier. The thought of self-love, or self-appreciation, or self-care wasn't even in my consciousness 'til the late 2010s, when I realised I was exhausting myself with this battle. I needed to stop fighting my body and allow it to be what it needed to be. I made a very conscious decision to make friends with it and learn to love it, no matter big or small. And I did.

So, with all this in mind, it is no wonder that we never stood a chance at being our own allies because we were never taught to be. But now, with a lot more of us becoming aware of this conditioning, we are reclaiming ourselves and learning to love ourselves again. And this is a wonderful thing because if we do not love ourselves or our body when it's well, how the hell are we going to love it when it's sick?! We therefore need to have more appreciation, gratitude and respect for it instead of disdain. We want to look at our bodies with awe and marvel at all the amazing things it does for us, rather than take it for granted and ridicule it.

It is no longer advisable to punish our body either physically or verbally, and when our body needs us the most (when it is sick) we need to be its best friend, aligning with it and caring for it. Sadly, it may take our body becoming sick before we register its significance in our life. When this happens, it is often the first time we realise how essential being well is and how our body is the vehicle for that wellness and wellbeing. So rather than fighting your body, I implore you to befriend it. Don't fight with it any longer. Even when you're feeling despondent and you're unwell, refrain from blaming it or being angry with it. If you want your body to heal, encourage it and be kind to it.

Exercise

Reflecting on this:
- » Think about the ways you were brought up, conditioned, or taught to fight with your body.
- » How did this affect your relationship with your body?

Reflections:

_____

_____

_____

_____

_____

_____

_____

_____

Now ask yourself:
- » Are you ready to commit to your body?
- » Are you willing to see your body as an ally and stop fighting it?
- » Will you offer it love and kindness?

If you answered **YES** to all of these then we can proceed to **Self-Commitment No. 2.**

~ Self-Commitment No. 2 ~
The Power of a Positive Mind—Positive Thoughts and Speech
What You Speak About, You Bring About

The second important element in the self-healing process is being exceptionally mindful of the **thoughts** and **words** you choose when thinking or speaking about: your body, your illness, where you are at in your life, and your life full stop!

THOUGHTS HAVE POWER! WORDS HAVE POWER!

I cannot stress enough how this is key to self-healing. Why? Because the way you speak about yourself, or your illness, will determine how your body responds to what you are thinking or saying. It will follow and respond to whatever it is you tell it or instruct it to do. *You* determine how it will respond—whether it follows your instructions to heal or not. *You* are in the driver's seat. *You* can influence your body simply by the thoughts and words *you* choose. This means that any negative thoughts about your body or illness need to be curtailed.

Anytime you think poorly of your situation, the illness, or your body, you must reframe it or rephrase it, or else you will simply continue to program it for illness. It's like you are programming your body to align with those negative thoughts you're sending out to it. If all you're telling it is that it is damaged or broken (or worse), then it responds by continuing to act that way. Every time you choose words that are low energetically (ones related to dark emotions, for example, the word **pain**), understand that it holds a low energetic vibration, and your body continues to respond by experiencing more pain. Try using more neutral words or more positive words. For example, use the word *discomfort* instead of pain. It's a great replacement. Or, instead of using the word illness try referring to it as *an experience or out of alignment*.

I believe *all* illnesses are just experiences and lessons. They exist because we are out of alignment and our body is showing us this. It's also giving us messages about where we are at and why we are having this experience. Nothing is random. We all attract into our lives experiences we need to learn from. Illnesses are just another form of this learning, except normally we don't see it that way. We tend to demonise them and victimise ourselves, feeling hopeless and powerless as a result. But we are not.

Back to the power of thoughts and words...

Before I understood this concept, I always used to get annoyed when people would say, "Be positive," if something bad was going on in my life, or if I wasn't well. I found it dismissive and judgmental, as though blaming me for my experience. And yet, in a way, I was to blame. Not in a sick, twisted, masochistic way, but rather that I was responsible. I had attracted this experience into my life and, by focusing on the negatives of the experience, I wasn't shifting it or clearing it. I was holding it to me rather than releasing it from me. I was aligning with the illness because I was focused on it and how it was negatively impacting my life, rather than finding a positive frame of reference for it and seeing my life as much more than just the things going wrong, or the illness.

Once I understood the concept and how I was responsible, I turned my focus instead towards all the things going well and right in my life. I was finding appreciation and gratitude for my life regardless of the illness, pain, or unfavourable situation I found myself in at that time. The whole time I was going through this experience, I only spoke kindly and supportively to my body. I would praise it every day. When the pain was unbearable, I would ask my body to let go of the anger it was carrying. As pain, heat, and inflammation is all about anger, or suppressed, unresolved, negative emotions, I would encourage my body to release the anger and explain how it was not serving that part of my body, or me, for that matter.

I would get up in the morning and be thankful that I could enjoy whatever the day was offering. I could do other things with my body. On the days where I was exhausted and not feeling uplifted or interested in much, I would allow myself to just *be* quiet. I would watch funny movies and read books that would take me away on adventures or give me wisdom to help me through the day. I would channel my focus into things that made my day better or I would rest if that was all I could do, never once giving myself a hard time for doing so. Understanding the process of healing means understanding that the body, on some days, will appear to regress or go backwards, but in fact it is just a part of the healing process. I had to 100% trust that all was well, even if I couldn't see it.

Avoiding using negative speech translates into helping your body heal. Refrain from using negative self-talk or thoughts that put yourself down. Self-monitor and call yourself to task when you find yourself speaking or thinking in a way that's hurtful and unhelpful, then reframe those words or thoughts into something more positive. It's all about finding appreciation in any given moment. Refer to your illness as a "temporary limitation" and remind yourself that you are learning something through it. You're *not* the sum of your illnesses or limitations and they're only a portion of you.

Positivity in this way is useful and encouraging. You're all about encouraging yourself and your body. You're all about building your body up and praising it, even when it appears to be out of whack or action. You let your body know how much you *love* and *appreciate* it for what it does for us, always believing in your body's ability to heal itself and *trusting* in your body's innate wisdom and knowledge. You're the guiding hand it requires along the way, and you must let it know that you're there, like a mother to a child, holding it and nurturing it with *love*. You never turn your back on it when the going gets tough, as though it's a lost cause.

Exercise

Reflect on this:
- » Think about how you have thought of, or spoken about, yourself, your body, or your illness in a negative way.
- » What ways can you speak, think or act in a more positive way in reference to yourself, your body or your illness?
- » In general, in what ways can you implement more positive thoughts, words and actions into your life?

Reflections:

_____

_____

_____

_____

_____

_____

_____

_____

Once your body knows you're committed to it and speaking to it with love and kindness, it cannot but respond. Now we can believe in ourselves and move on to **Self-Commitment No. 3**.

~ Self-Commitment No. 3 ~
Do You Believe?
Challenging and Replacing Limiting Beliefs

The third important commitment in the self-healing journey is **believing**: in the power of self, in the body's ability to heal, in a higher power to assist, and that anything is possible. Can you fully believe in something you can't see, measure or quantify? Can you believe even when you can't see evidence of any healing taking place and trusting that it *is* taking place?

Believing without **seeing**. This is the real test. However, it is also about recognising any limiting belief systems that you may have unconsciously programmed, which hinder or restrict your ability to believe in your self-healing. Stay with me—this may be a little confusing, but it will be perfectly clear in the end.

First, we have to believe in ourselves. This means we must **believe** in our ability to heal and trust that we are doing the healing. Secondly, believing is crucial in accepting that we are not always in charge of how things are going to manifest or transpire. We must surrender that part to **Source**. We can't control the full process, but it's about knowing we have followed the process: we've set our intention, we've been attentive to ourselves, mindful of our thoughts and words, and offered praise and kindness to our body, we've focused on what we wish the desired outcome to be—that we are healed, and then we **believe** that it *is* done. The healing is completed. We are **healed**!

We must trust that although we can't **see** what's happening yet, we believe that it is occurring. It *is* in the process of manifesting. The body may not show signs of healing straight away even though it *is* in the process of it. The manifestation will be revealed in time. Believe in self, the body, and the power of **Source** to deliver the desired outcome.

What If We Don't Believe in Any of This?
It is likely that we are experiencing limiting belief systems. Somewhere in our life, we have been conditioned or programmed to not believe in these things—in our abilities as powerful healers, in the body's innate ability to heal, and in **Source** to assist us.

You may also believe that you:
- are not worthy or deserving of healing
- deserve to be unwell or ill
- are being punished for something and/or deserve to be punished
- are paying something back, perhaps karmic debt
- need to suffer because this is part of the human experience
- are redeemed through suffering
- don't deserve to live in full alignment and in full wellness
- will get sick because it is expected as part of ageing or because of genetics/ancestry, and just accept it
- are only human with limited abilities.

These are some of the more common limiting beliefs that clients identify with. Can you see how latching onto any of these beliefs or programs creates a resistance to healing and well-being?

I recall when seeing the doctor regarding my mystery illness, she had pointed out that I was about the right age to expect to have arthritis manifest, alluding to this as a possible diagnosis because it was a genetic condition my mother had been diagnosed with. The first thing I thought was: I do not believe that I will have this condition just because my mother did. I do not believe it will manifest just because I'm at the age that it is expected to manifest. It is not a given; it is *not* how my story goes. And that was the commitment and conviction I had in that moment before I even had time to really consider what I'd just said and the implications of it. I was decreeing out loud that I was in charge. It also meant that I was going to need to back myself now.

I mean, what was the worst-case scenario? I got sicker? I lost my legs so I couldn't walk at all? I died? All these ran through my head as the "what if" scenarios when I was turning my back on conventional medical treatment and walking out of the doctor's surgery. How could I be so arrogant or stupid? But deep inside my heart, I *knew* with all conviction that I had this. I would prove to myself, and to the doctor, that I could heal without medical intervention, and I would no longer have any residual disease in my body the next time she tested me.

As a *waiver clause*, I accepted right there and then full responsibility for the outcome. I said to **Source**, "If this is what you want for me then I accept and I will not blame anyone, not even myself. I will accept whatever the outcome is, and never regret my decision to reject medical interference and do this on my own. I am fully committed to the decision I've made to take charge of my body's healing regardless of the outcome—desirable or undesirable—but I still believe I have the power with your help to do this."

There's a feeling of power that descends upon you when you are so aligned with the belief in your body's ability to heal, in your ability to assist it, and in the guidance of **Source** to help you along the way. It feels surreal but magical. Knowing you can do this even though you don't know the **how** is very empowering. Then you get to work believing that:

ANYTHING IS POSSIBLE
and that
YOU CAN DO IT!

All of the limiting beliefs can be released, and new beliefs created and programmed in to replace them. None of them are set in stone. None of them need to manifest in unwellness. *All* are only in existence as long as you **believe** in them. You can switch these out at any time. You have the power!

What you need to do is identify what those limiting beliefs, or belief systems, are and change them. Part of the self-healing process is about reprogramming these beliefs so that you come into full alignment with wellbeing. *You* don't want to stand in the way of your self-healing because deep down you hold beliefs that misalign with the creation and manifestation of wellness and wellbeing. This will counter any attempt to heal yourself. It's like talking the talk but not believing in what you're saying, or you're self-sabotaging, so always be mindful of what your beliefs are. They are either wonderful supporters or destructive opponents of your life.

Exercise

Reflect on this:
- » Do you believe you can be healed?
- » Can you identify any blocks to believing this is possible?
- » Are there any other things preventing you from trusting or believing that healing and wellbeing is possible?
- » What can you do to help yourself learn more about the power of belief and how to implement it in your life?

Reflections:

~~~~~~

~~~~~~

~~~~~~

~~~~~~

~~~~~~

~~~~~~

~~~~~~

~~~~~~

Are you ready to release your fears and start believing? This brings us to **Self-Commitment No. 4**.

~ Self-Commitment No. 4 ~
No Fear
Releasing Any Fear of the Unknown

The fourth important self-commitment is releasing all fear, the most crippling of all emotions humans can experience. It robs us from living our lives fully. I'm not talking about the kind of fear you experience when you're in a dangerous situation or emergency and need to get into fight or flight mode. That is what fear is there for: to help you activate your nervous system and your adrenal glands (adrenaline) to do whatever you need to do to get out of the presenting situation and protect yourself. Fear can also be a body's way of alerting you to the dangers of impending events, like jumping out of a plane. If you're doing this for recreation, then you're choosing to override this natural response and tap into the adrenaline rush, which is translated as fun.

However, fear can become a disorder if you let it control you. It can manifest as anxiety, which is crippling and debilitating, and can prevent you from engaging in life. If you only focus on the possible negative outcomes of a situation, then you leave no room for the positive possibilities to manifest. You therefore live constantly in fear of the future, trying to predict the unpredictable. Nothing feels safe and you no longer trust life as a result of this, sabotaging all opportunities for joy and fun. This is what happened to me. I was living in fear due to a mental illness.

I suffered from anxiety on and off throughout my life, and learning to self-regulate and self-soothe meant that I needed to find a way to curtail the fear aspect that is related to anxiety. This is usually fear:
- of the future
- of the unknown
- of being out of control, and/or
- that things will not work out.

To heal myself from this affliction, I had to learn to live in the present. I had to learn that I could trust myself and the Universe, and that all would be well in the end. I had to learn to remain centred whenever I felt a situation was out of my control. In many ways, I had to learn to surrender and accept that I would always be looked after, and that nothing would ever be given to me that I could not handle.

Arriving at this place changed everything for me. It meant that when I was faced with a potentially unknown or indefinite outcome, instead of becoming anxious and panicked, I was able to remain calm knowing that I would be okay. This came with spiritual practice and spiritual awareness, mostly through meditation and listening to positively affirming spiritual teachers, such as Esther and Jerry Hicks, and Louise Hay [9]. I stopped being fearful of the unknown and the fact I couldn't control everything. I felt safe and secure in my knowing and everything in my life became easier, especially when I was faced with an illness that had an indefinite outcome.

How is All This Applicable?
Think about what you would do if you were given a serious diagnosis (if you haven't already got one). Your initial reaction generally comes from a place of fear. You may even go into a state of panic, which could spiral into a state of helplessness and despair. All your power ebbs away, leaving you feeling vulnerable and a victim. Suddenly, you're reviewing your life and the impact this illness is potentially going to have on all areas of it. It's like there's a switch that turns on saying, "**Impending doom on the horizon**".

But what if, instead of coming from a place of fear and powerlessness upon receiving a critical diagnosis, you feel in charge of the situation? You realise you are not at the mercy of the diagnosis but have potential power over it to activate your own healing. How incredibly wonderful would that be? Everything is possible.

---

9 See Appendix II for recommendations

And don't forget...
You are not alone on this healing journey. Working with **Source** means your healing is front and centre. Once you establish that connection and trust that you are being held during this time, you know that you do not walk alone. I mean, after all, you are tapping into the best in the healing business!

Exercise

Reflect on this:
- » Think about when you've found yourself feeling anxious or fearful when faced with a serious situation or illness in your life. Were you able to centre yourself? If so, how did you do this?
- » If not, think about what you could do if faced with it again?
- » Are there practices or methods you could implement in your life now to help you overcome your fears and master your own centre?

Reflections:

That brings us to **Self-Commitment No. 5**.

~ Self-Commitment No. 5 ~
Trusting Source
Giving Up Control and Surrendering to a Higher Purpose

We come to the fifth important self-commitment: to *trust* in a higher power. Whether you want to call this power **Source** (my preference), **God**, **Universe**, **Higher Energy**, **Supreme Being**, or **The ALL** then this is the energy you will be tapping into. This essence will be channelled through you when applying the healing technique. This superior **all-knowing** energy will be working its way through you when you're doing your healing. It will also be to whom, or to what, you'll surrender once you've done the work. We're always working with the highest of the High. Why go to the spirits, angels, archangels etc., when you can go directly to the top? I never work with lower-level beings or spirits, or even superior ones; I only work with **Source**.

Over the years, through my spiritual journey and practice, I figured out that God was not some elusive figure that I could only talk to if I was praying (in the traditional sense) or, if I was in church, through a third-party self-appointed representative. I became aware that casually dialoguing with Source in my home or out in nature in a quiet, meditative or reflective state connected me immediately. You see, it's the *intention* not the *ritual* that connects you to Source. Now, I have a direct line to Source and so can you. You'll learn to initiate one.

It is *essential* to establish this connection or contact with Source for the healing relationship to be activated. You must be able to commune directly with Source to ask for what you want. It's a dialogue between the both of you. When I was learning the technique, I was communicating all the time during my daily meditation practice—asking questions, asking for clarity if I didn't know, asking for insights, asking how to ask correctly. All this was done as if we were in the same room together discussing my healing and what was best. This is what working with Source is like. He is not some distant patriarchal figure that's out of reach. **He/She, Father/Mother, God** is right here, right now.

When you learn to work with Source, you'll surrender to the fact that you are essentially a passenger. I know it sounds contrary to what I've been saying—that **you** are in charge of healing yourself—and that is true, but you'll appreciate that Source has all the power and wants so much to assist you. You are channelling that power through you as the vessel for receiving this healing power. You are asking Source to do the healing on you whilst you are the receiver. Even if it feels like you're doing the healing on yourself, you are not alone. You are being worked through. Once you learn the technique later in the **9 Steps Part IV**, it'll become clearer.

There will come a time when you'll have to let Source do the driving. You'll be required to be patient, surrender yourself and let Her take charge of completing the work. This may be challenging if you like to be in control of everything in your life because this will not always be up to you to direct. It's like teamwork—you ask for the healing to be done, you activate the process, and then you sit back and *allow* **Source** to do the rest by bringing it into manifestation.

It's all about creating and manifesting: creating the body you wish to exist in and then allowing it to come to fruition in **divine timing**—manifesting into the present time and reality. You are drawing the healed version of yourself down from the higher dimensions where everything you have ever wished for exists and is waiting for you to pull it through into the third dimension. Your job during this time is to trust that all will manifest in good time. That the healing is done. What you think about and dream about, you bring about. All you do is focus on the outcome—**wellness and wellbeing**. The moment you stop believing or trusting and getting in your own way, the whole process can be sabotaged. Everything can slip back in an instant.

Imagine you're watching a tiny seed growing. You planted it and you know instinctively that it needs to be left alone in the dark where you can't see what's happening, yet you trust that it is growing under there. All you do is nurture it and try to keep its environment as suitable as possible. You don't keep uncovering the soil to look at the seed and see where it's up to. You don't disturb it at all. You just leave it alone to do its thing. Eventually, when the seed is ready, it will break through the surface of the soil making its progress more visible.

It's the same with healing. You don't keep interfering. You don't get impatient and keep questioning when you're going to get there. You simply trust the process is taking place even if you can't see it take place. Like the seed, your healing will burst through the darkness into the light making it visible to you in Source's time. You just need to be patient, surrender and trust.

Exercise

Reflect on this:
- » Do you have a preferred method of communicating with Source?
- » Do you trust Source with assisting you?
- » Are you willing to surrender and let go of control?
- » If you struggle to let go or trust, are you willing to learn this?
- » In which ways, or what things, can you do to help yourself be more trusting?

Reflections:

_____

_____

_____

_____

_____

_____

_____

_____

Let's now proceed to **Self-Commitment No. 6**.

~ Self-Commitment No. 6 ~
Meditation Practice
A Way to Access the Theta State for Hearing Guidance and Healing the Body

The sixth important commitment is **meditation** practice. Most people use meditation for relaxation, to quieten the mind, to destress the body, and to have a break in the day where there is some peace. In this healing process, however, meditation is used as a portal for communicating with **Source**, hearing the messages your body is revealing, and for instructing the healing to be done. It is far more of an active, rather than passive, meditation practice. Yet it is still a peaceful process—calming for the body and mind, just in a very different way.

I find visualisation meditations are the best way to assist you to train yourself to *see, hear, sense* your way around your body. These meditations activate all your senses, like going to the seaside, or a forest, or a different time or place. These are the *go-to* meditations I recommend if you want to tune yourself up for self-healing, because you're going to be doing a lot of visualising, listening and sensing. And to be honest, I find this type of meditation practice more fun.

Meditation is the only way to bring yourself into the quietness required for the conscious mind to recede, and to allow space for the subconscious, or **Higher Self**, to come forth. Meditation is generally experienced in the state of alpha—the slowed down relaxation state. However, in the *Metaphysical Healing Meditations (MHMs)* you'll be learning to access the state of theta, which lies between alpha and delta (the sleep state). It's a much deeper, trance-like state (as in hypnosis), where you can access all information and all knowing. It is a way for you to tap into the greater aspect of yourself, the bigger part of you beyond the veil, and communicate directly with **Source**.

Over my lifetime, I have used different methods to find what suits me best. Of course, I haven't meditated religiously throughout my life (I'm not that disciplined) but I do use it regularly to centre myself if I'm feeling out of alignment. I also use walking as a meditation practice or contemplation tool, and I do this almost daily. Nature works wonders for me, and I'd rather be outdoors meditating than in a room with four walls. I find even just quietly sitting in the forest automatically transforms my mental state, putting me into a calm and quiet mood.

I have often taken groups of people out into the forest or to the ocean to practice this form of meditation. It's especially useful, and I highly recommend it for those who struggle to meditate or to get into a quiet state. This way, they just have to be still and take in all that's surrounding them, activating all their senses. Nothing beats nature to help you relax.

When I was healing myself, I would meditate at four o'clock in bed every morning for about an hour. I didn't plan it that way. It just happened that I would naturally awaken around that time due to the pain waves kicking in. Initially, I was annoyed at waking early like this and being in so much pain, but I soon realised it was an opportunity to work on my pain early to help me get through the day ahead. Any time where I was well enough to drive down to the ocean or be near nature, I would take my deck chair or stay seated in my car and meditate there. This served as a multiple therapy opportunity: fresh air, vitamin D, observing nature, being quiet, meditating, and reflecting, all in one hit. It was definitely medicine to me, and I'd prescribe it to anyone to do the same.

My meditation practice initially became all about focusing on my legs to relieve the pain and reduce the swelling. I would put all my intentions and energy into each knee using my hands as heat packs. It's incredible how hot your hands can get when you use them as healing tools. It's like they switch on when you activate them for healing while meditating. This was one of the incredible discoveries I made during these times: my hands were heat tools.

I began using my hands for heat packing at night when sleeping. My hands would reach furnace-like temperatures and the heat around my knees would be soaring. I would be sweating like I was in a sauna; it was incredible! I know some of it was probably due to my own temperature being high due to illness, but the extra heat was driving all the nasties out, sweating them out. I knew it was killing whatever illness, virus or bacteria was present in my body. I intuitively realised that nothing could withstand this kind of heat. I was healing my body whilst killing these entities with the incredible amounts of heat being generated out of my hands!

For your information, the hands have Chakras (energy centres) in them which are associated with the Heart Chakra. This meditation practice is heart-centred, so it's no wonder this energy permeates through all parts of us, especially through our hands. We can heal with our hands, just as Jesus did. When we are connected to our heart, this energy is directed out through our hands into those receiving healing from us, or in this case, into ourselves.

I digress a little but for good reason because the practice of meditation allowed me to access this divine knowledge. It was like a portal for this *Divine Instruction* to come through as intuition. When I'd receive any information that was "foreign" to me, I'd usually investigate the meaning of it to get more insight. Google is great for finding information out or directing you to good reference material. That's how I found out about the Chakras in our hands being connected to the Heart Chakra. I talk more about the Chakras in **Appendix I**.

Meditation is really such a valuable spiritual tool. It doesn't just offer quiet time, but an opportunity to discover wonderful spiritual and esoteric information and ultimately, a portal to healing ourselves. It's a one stop shop of magic.

Meditation is a wonderful tool for the mind and spirit, but I also needed to take care of the physical aspect of my body. So, whilst I used meditation for pain relief and healing, I also looked into how I could properly nourish and boost my body with nutrition.

Exercise

Reflect on this:
- » Do you meditate?
- » If so, where do you prefer to meditate?
- » Are there any obstacles to meditation?
- » Are you willing to learn a method that works for you and/or practice regularly?

Reflections:

_____

_____

_____

_____

_____

_____

_____

_____

Nourishing and boosting my body with nutrition is where **Self-Commitment No.7** comes into focus.

~ Self-Commitment No. 7 ~
Provide a Supportive Environment
Choosing Things That Support my Body's Recovery

Setting Up a Supportive Environment for Your Body
I would like you to imagine this Self-commitment as setting up your environment so that it supports your **self-healing** process. These things could be, for example:
- diet
- exercise
- health supplements and remedies
- pampering or remedial treatments
- alternative pain reduction methods
- attending wellness retreats and/or
- creating a less stressful environment in your home.

This Self-commitment may seem less significant than the others, but it is worth taking note. There may be some valuable insights that you may not have considered previously.

No pills, just good food
During my self-healing journey, I had taken very little in the way of painkillers because, as mentioned previously, they made me nauseous. But I still wanted to find alternative ways that were non-toxic to assist with reducing the pain. Heat packing my knees constantly, day and night, was very effective in reducing the aches in them. Initially, I assumed that heat packing would be counterintuitive, but in fact, when I tried the alternative (cold packing) it was instant agony. I experimented with lotions, ointments and supplements 'til I found the magic remedy for myself. Out of the many lotions and rubs I tried, only one worked for me—a good old-fashioned ointment we used to have in the medicine cabinet when I was a child.

Investigating food and nutrition was important to me because I'd seen how it assisted others on their wellness journeys. I researched the benefits of certain diets and foods and how they played a part in boosting my immunity. Essentially, food is medicine and can assist in supporting your body's self-healing. It is something positive that adds value in your life, plus it is easy to do and available everywhere. More specifically, I discovered how certain types of foods were more acidic and, therefore, likely to trigger inflammation. I realised that if I wanted to reduce pain in my body, I needed to reduce the inflammation. Reducing inflammation meant changing my diet from acidic to more alkaline. Thus, choosing foods that were more alkaline meant I was supporting my body's environment naturally.

I was fortunate to have a family acquaintance who understood diet as a way to support health. He recommended that I investigate the role of the lymphatic system in helping the body clear toxins from the bloodstream. Lymphatic health is key to assisting the body's natural detox mechanism. He also suggested that I listen to Doctor Robert Morse, a naturopathic physician and expert on the lymphatic system and its role in keeping the body healthy and harmonious. Although he may be considered controversial to mainstream medicine, with 50 years of research under his belt, I felt he was a credible and worthy source of information. I followed his protocols and turned my body from acidic to alkaline, which I believe was a critical element in my body's recovery.

NOTE: I'm not a dietician or nutritionist, so don't just accept my word for what to put in your body. This information is based on my own investigation and with the assistance of someone more knowledgeable in the area of healing the body with food than I am. I advise you to do your own investigative research and seek guidance from someone knowledgeable in either alternative or traditional aspects of nutrition with whom you resonate.

Move it
I feel exercise is another valuable component in supporting your body's recovery. Although I was unable to exercise when I was ill, it is still an area worthwhile considering. Exercise offers so many benefits, such as increasing endorphins in your brain and stimulating oxygen flowing through your body. You may be limited

in the ways you can exercise but it may be the kind of support mentally, if not physically, you're looking for.

Treat yourself

Other helpful ways to support your body and your mind simultaneously are treatments such as:
- massage (relaxation or remedial)
- saunas
- aromatherapy
- acupuncture
- reiki
- sound healing
- crystal healing
- light therapy.

There are so many types of wellness-promoting modalities that assist your body and mind because, with a calm, relaxed mind and body, you are better able to face or deal with your illness.

Exercise
Reflect on this:
- » Are you willing to investigate and implement changes to your environment in order to support your wellness? Make a list of the ways or actions you'd like to do this.
- » Are there any other methods or actions not mentioned in this chapter you think would be beneficial?

Reflections:

~~~~~~

~~~~~~

~~~~~~

~~~~~~

~~~~~~

~~~~~~

~~~~~~

From providing a supportive environment to a chance to repair, it's time to give your body the rest it deserves. This brings us to **Self-Commitment No. 8.**

~ Self-Commitment No. 8 ~
Resting, Resting and More Resting

For most of my life, I was conditioned to believe that illness was something to push through and ignore. Unless I was dying, I would simply "soldier on". I even remember the television and radio ads promoting this very notion from medication companies. They made it seem so valiant and noble for you to get up and fight through your illness, as though going to work under these conditions made you a hero for doing so. It was simply unacceptable to stay home and rest; maybe a day or two of this would suffice, but any longer made me feel guilty. It was as if staying home to recover was somehow indulgent and luxurious. Whether going to school or work, I would take my pills and just get on with it, sharing my cold and flu bugs as I went along. I'm sure you can relate.

The irony of this warped conditioning—to get better by pushing through it—is that it is counterintuitive to healing yourself, not to mention delusional. If you truly wished to recover properly, you'd give yourself permission to rest and not feel guilty or frustrated about it. Healing takes place when you are resting because during rest you are reducing interference with your body/body part, giving it space to feel safe to recover. You are disrespecting your body by continuing to go against its natural requirement to rest so that healing can take place. You are putting your body into resistance mode rather than allowing it to align with its desire to heal.

In my process of healing, resting was an intricate part of this. I would never force myself to keep going against my body's desire to sleep or lay there. I know it's challenging to just let the days pass by without being an active participant, but sometimes you must take a back seat. On the days I couldn't get out of bed, I let myself be there without being angry or frustrated. I accepted my body's request to rest, never pushed or forced it against its will, and I respected it. In return, it healed.

You see, your body will tell you when it's ready for you to start moving around or exercising the parts that are damaged, or to push a little through the resistance to bring it back to recovery. If you listen, your body guides you; it instructs you on what to do and how to proceed. So, for the best outcome when healing yourself, rest is prescribed. You must make yourself a priority and, for rest to work, you need patience with your body and yourself.

Exercise

Reflect on this:
- » What's your view on "resting"?
- » Do you find it acceptable to rest as part of your healing?
- » Do you feel any resistance around resting?
- » What challenges do you have, if any, around the concept of resting for recovery?
- » Are you willing to accept rest as part of your recovery?

Reflections:

_____

_____

_____

_____

_____

_____

_____

_____

Now we reach **Self-Commitment No. 9**.

~ Self-Commitment No. 9 ~
Patience
No Deadlines or Time Frames

I constantly prayed to have more patience in my life; I feel it is such a desirable quality. But patience took a while to meet me, instead, coming in the form of my daughter who has much more patience than I ever did. I was eventually given the gift of patience during my healing experience. Patience may be one of your greatest obstacles, yet with time, perhaps your greatest achievement because, along with all the resting you will be required to do, you will need a lot of patience.

When healing yourself, your patience may be tested due to:
- all the resting you'll be doing
- being inactive
- not feeling or seeing change quickly
- having no certainty, only uncertainty and unpredictability, and
- not knowing how long it will take to completely heal.

It's not like going to the doctor, receiving an estimated timeframe in which to expect healing to occur, and even then, it's never guaranteed. If you have the flu, traditionally you're given antibiotics and told it should clear in a week. If it doesn't, then you feel there's something wrong with you and you may panic. You may return to the doctor questioning the prognosis and asking for more antibiotics or more tests. Your doctor may tell you to go home to rest more and return in a week if it's not cleared. On it goes 'til it either clears of its own accord or you keep returning to the doctor to be tested again and again, certain you've been misdiagnosed. During this process, you've relied on a system of treatment and a projected outcome that should, in your understanding, deliver the results you are hoping for in a speedy timeframe. Because that's what you're expecting: a fast recovery so your life is not disrupted for long.

What you may not have considered in this equation is that your body actually required *more* time to heal. Perhaps it was your unwillingness to slow down and rest that slowed the healing process. Instead, you've relied on an external influence to provide an outcome that is inorganic to your body, when perhaps all that was required was more rest and the acceptance and patience that accompanies it. Often *quick fixes* are not applicable when your body heals organically. Even if you are using medications, your body will not always follow the doctor's prescription, but you can assist it further along its healing journey by being willing to explore this for yourself with patience and courage.

When I was healing myself, I was acutely aware of my own expectations of an outcome. I wanted to see something happening with all the work I was doing. I remember thinking, "Oh it's been three months already and I'm still not seeing much change." But the reality was, there were tiny progresses every single day, they just weren't big noticeable ones. I learned to become super sensitive to even the tiniest of improvements and I'd hold onto that.

Another thing I learned was that looking at how long it'd been did not help me. In fact, it created worry and stress for me, and nervousness. I also realised that by engaging in those worries and fears, I automatically halted any progress I was making because I was focusing on the negatives, attracting *more* of what I didn't want. It's like spinning a wheel: you spin it and spin it, the momentum is growing and the speed's increasing, but the moment you apply even a tiny bit of pressure to it, it slows down, eventually grinding to halt. Healing is like that. There's momentum building and building behind the scenes, and eventually it can hold its own but the moment you start getting impatient and expecting things to be a certain way, you slow the process down. Your thoughts are impacting the momentum.

Now, I'd like to challenge you to notice when next you're ill how you behave. Really take notice of:
- your thoughts
- your expectations

- how willing you are to spend time resting
- how patient or impatient you are
- how frustrated with yourself you are, and
- how fearful or worried you get.

Be present, honest and open-minded enough to explore the possibility that you may be an impatient person who's going to learn to be patient. By being patient, not "a patient", you are allowing the behind-the-scenes work to begin to reveal itself.

Be patient and trust healing is happening. **Believe** that it is happening. Then **see** it actually manifest in its **divine** timing. Healing is all about divine **timing**. Let the Universe take charge. It *is* responding to your efforts and your vibration. Knowing that, just sit back and relax. Find joy in the experience because joy can be found regardless of your challenges.

Exercise
Reflect on this:
- » Do you consider yourself a patient person?
- » What challenges do you experience when required to be patient?
- » How do these affect you?
- » What methods or practices can you implement to help you be more patient?

Reflections:

_____

_____

_____

_____

_____

_____

_____

This brings us to the final **Self-Commitment No. 10**.

~ Self-Commitment No. 10 ~
Be Present
Live in the NOW. Enjoy Life

I've said it before: you are not the sum of your illness. One of the first things I notice when I am in the presence of people who are unwell is that they tend to only focus on the illness. They are consumed with reviewing and relaying in detail every aspect of their illness: symptoms, doctor/specialist visits, medications, daily routine, and so on. Almost everything else they have ever known or ever were ceases to exist. They stop doing things they like or things that bring them joy and focus only on the suffering aspect. Not only that but they stop seeing possibilities in their lives, only their limitations. I know it sounds harsh but it's like they become consumed with their illness and own it—**it's MY illness**. Suddenly that's all they become, and yet it's just one aspect of themselves. It is not their totality but it's that aspect that becomes their total focus and identity. They *identify* as the illness and limitation.

I know it's challenging to be positive and not become obsessed with your illness, especially when you're in pain or experiencing restrictions in your life. But it's important to detach from *becoming* **the illness** instead of just experiencing it. I made certain that the part of my body that was in limitation did not dictate the whole of me. I still had many body parts that weren't disrupted, and it was in my best interests to focus on them. By giving them more of my attention, I began to see what those parts could offer me and how they could be of benefit to me, even while my legs were experiencing restriction. I was essentially retraining myself by focusing on the positive aspects of my body instead of being consumed by the negative aspects of it. I couldn't walk. I was in pain. But what could I do to find joy in my day?

I began by looking at my legs and thinking about their function, and what aspects of them made me happy. My legs are about walking, being mobile. But what was it about walking that made me happy?

What exactly did it mean to me? What were the benefits I was getting from it? I needed to break it into down to its components.

Walking meant freedom to move about, being outdoors, and enjoying nature and fresh air. It was also about fitness and relaxation. Walking was a meditation practice that assisted with my mental health and physical wellbeing. It was a mood uplifter. In summary, walking meant a lot of things to me that I was now missing out on because I couldn't do it. The key, then, was finding a way to access some of these benefits walking gave me without being able to do so. Out of all these benefits, only **movement** was limited at this time. I could still access all the other benefits, I just had to access them in a different way; that is, bypass or go around the limitation. Easy!

Next came identifying how I wanted to implement those benefits in an easily accessible way. I thought about the places that made me feel the happiest when out walking: the beach or the forest. These places offered me peace, calm, joy, connection to nature, and relaxation. The beauty was I could access all these benefits in one hit just by going to these places. Better yet, I could still receive them and experience them even if I couldn't walk.

On the days where the pain was too great or I was too tired to go anywhere, I'd graciously surrender and stay home, reading and writing. I read for escape, disappearing into fantastical stories or daydreams, or for learning, educating myself in new and wonderful ways. Every day was an opportunity to do something. Although not huge things, they were still ways for me to enjoy my day regardless of experiencing limitation. While the rest of my body was functioning, why not focus on those parts and do the best I could with them instead? I simply refocused my attention on what I *could* do rather than on what I couldn't.

This is such a revelation! Discovering the power you can have over your situation, no matter what you are experiencing, means you can quite easily choose an enjoyable time over a miserable one. It doesn't matter if it's a short-term or long-term illness, all you need to do is make the most of what is happening in the present moment of each day. Finding joy in your day wherever possible is your goal.

Exercise
Reflect on this:
- » Identify the areas in your life or in your body where you are experiencing limitation and restriction. Why is it so important to you and how does it benefit you?
- » How else can you access those benefits even if faced with this limitation or restriction?
- » What will you do to bring more positive aspects and joy into your day?

Reflections:

~ Reflecting on the Self-Commitments ~

This section has provided you with a way to become more aligned with your body and become its ally. Through these **Self-Commitments**, you are ensuring a greater alliance with your body so that healing will take place. Before we finalise this section and move on, I'd like you to reflect on it overall. This will give you the opportunity to look back on all that's been discussed to see what you've learned and how it benefits you.

Exercise
- » After going through this section, how do you feel about committing to your body?
- » Which of these Self-Commitments do you feel challenges you the most?
- » What will you do to remedy this?
- » What other commitments to your body or yourself have you thought of that may not have been mentioned here?

Reflections:

~~~~~~

~~~~~~

~~~~~~

~~~~~~

~~~~~~

~~~~~~

Part IV
~ The Metaphysical Healing Meditations ~

~ By Divine Instruction ~
Learning the Metaphysical Healing Meditations

The healing process was not an overnight revelation. The information was drip fed to me every night through my meditation practice over a period of seven months as a series of *Divine Instructions*. When I began, I was using the methods I'd been taught as a ThetaHealer. This was to be a great learning platform from which to build on. However, through this regular connection with Source I began receiving new and more in-depth *Divine Instructions* spoken to me in a way I could understand. In this way, I was taught additional information pertaining to the healing process and its essential components. I gained a deeper, fuller understanding of what was required for successful and complete healing.

It was revealed to me that the healing process is made up of several steps, or layers, with each step needing to be addressed and attended to for the presenting issue to be resolved. Each of the steps asks you to work through something and each one is essential to address in order to move onto the next one. If one step isn't addressed, chances are you may be better but not completely recovered or well, indicating that there is still something requiring attention. The best part is your body tells you everything you need to know so you can gauge where you are at. The trick is learning how to listen to your body and learning what it's telling you.

Learning what your body is telling you is something you need to tune into. I had the skills and the time to work it out on my own; however, for many of you this is new. But I'm certain you'll learn how to listen to your own body and work out what messages it's sending you. There are books available that have done some of the hard work already, giving you a head start on the healing process (see **Appendix II** for recommendations, particularly Julia Cannon and Louise Hay). As you progress and develop your own abilities, you'll be able to understand what your body is saying without referring to other books but access them if you wish.

The process of learning the *Metaphysical Healing Meditations (MHMs)* has been broken down for you into the Steps, which you address individually. There are 9 Steps to complete healing.

~ The Step-by-Step Guide ~

9 Steps to Complete Healing

Step 1 ~ Getting into the **Theta** state and connecting to a Higher Power.

Step 2 ~ How to do a **Body Scan** and notice where issues are.

Step 3 ~ How to apply the **healing blue light**.

Step 4 ~ How to listen to and **decipher the messages** your body is revealing to you.

Step 5 ~ Identifying your limiting **belief systems** and replacing them.

Step 6 ~ Understanding **ancestral/genetic** illnesses and clearing them.

Step 7 ~ How to communicate with your **DNA** and switch ON/OFF genetic markers.

Step 8 ~ Communicating with the **cells** in your body.

Step 9 ~ **Forgiveness** work.

Each step is as important as the next and best carried out in sequence. However, you do not have to do all these steps in one sitting. In fact, it is often better to do one step at a time, then take a break. When learning this technique, it is recommended to try one step and practice it a little so that you build your confidence. The first step is the key to the rest of them, so take your time. When I do my own healing work, depending on the severity of the issue, I tend to work through one step a day to give each layer a chance to integrate before moving onto the next step. If it's only something small, I may move quickly through the whole series of steps in one sitting. At times, I may repeat or revisit a certain step if I feel there's a little resistance around that area.

Once you learn the technique and become confident with it, you'll intuitively know what to do and what works best for you. Each time will be different and will require your discretion as to how best to proceed. Some days it'll be easy, and you'll find you are really focused. Other days, you may find it a little more difficult to focus or **drop into Theta**. I find that these days, when your mind is elsewhere and you're too distracted or have a lot on your mind, it is best to leave it and return to it when you're in the right headspace or mood.

Try not to force yourself to do healing work or force a session onto yourself; you'll find you're more likely to get frustrated and not enjoy the process. Take your time, be present and be in no rush to get it done. Remember to be patient and gentle with yourself, and trust that it's always in **divine timing**.

Best Practice
Before you begin your healing session, find a comfortable place to either sit or lay down where it is quiet so you will not be disturbed. I love to lay down in/on my bed. My favourite time is in the early morning before I get up and out of bed when I'm quiet and receptive. But I can do a healing session anywhere. I love to do this outdoors while sitting at the beach, or in the forest with my back up against a tree. I find nature to be very supportive in the healing process. Whatever works for you, just do that.

*NOTE: I do not recommend putting music on because this is a distraction and can keep you in an Alpha state rather than dropping into the deeper Theta state. I'll explain further.

Theta is the state required for this healing. It is the gateway to connecting directly with our **Higher Selves** and with Source. We are communing with the higher realms. Theta is the state between Alpha, the relaxed state in which most meditations and energy work is done—Reiki, for instance, is operating in the Alpha state—and Delta, the sleep state. Theta lies between the two, right before we drift off to sleep. We may be in a semiconscious state and begin to experience waves of images appearing, often in abstract form. It is also the state accessed during a hypnosis session. Often clients will report being aware of where they are, yet still able to access the subconscious mind (the High Self mind), such as when viewing their past lives.

Theta is a very powerful state where you can accomplish remarkable things and have access to a greater knowledge than you ever thought possible. It is truly the portal between the present, the past and the future. It is also the link between that which lies beyond the veil in the higher dimensions. From here, you can access Source directly and open up to the universal cosmic consciousness. It is here that healing takes place and is then drawn down into the present to manifest in the Third Dimension. Miracles do happen and magic really does exist, you just have to know how to access it.

You will be required to do a lot of visualising, essentially activating the right side of your brain. It may take some practice and getting used to. Trust what you are seeing and allow the images to come to you. Practice some visualisation meditations to help you. For example, imagine you're going to the beach or the forest and notice as much detail as possible. You can even imagine walking through your house, going through each room, noticing every detail. This is an excellent way to get familiar with visualising.
*NOTE: If you have difficulty visualising (seeing in your mind's eye), or if you suffer from Aphantasia (a lack of mental imagery), try **sensing** by listening or feeling.

Recommendation for How to Get the Best Out of the Meditations
- Read each meditation step through first so you understand what you're doing and why.
- Record yourself reading the meditation part of these steps.
- Read them slowly with breaks in between to allow for the steps to be followed while you have your eyes closed.
- Listen to your own voice-recorded meditation guidance to help you get used to the process.
- Do this for all your steps.

NOTE: Voice recording apps are available for your mobile phone. The iPhone has a Voice Memos app already included in the Utilities section. It's great and I have used this myself many times. I'm sure other phones have similar apps, or else you can download a new one, use a handheld digital recorder or even your computer.

~ STEP 1 ~
Getting Into the Theta State and Connecting to a Higher Power

The very first thing you'll do to start every meditation is connect to **Source/God/Universe**. For best results, choose one reference and stick to it. I will use Source throughout.

Connecting to Source is the most important aspect of the healing process. Why? Because you are the instrument and the vehicle for healing and you're not working alone. You're accessing a far greater power to channel through you for healing. And why use anything or anyone else when you can go directly to the Source! In order to access this connection, you need to drop into the powerful Theta state, the state of higher consciousness.

As part of your meditations, you're also going to be *asking* for what you want. You must not be afraid to be direct and clear. The words you choose are important, so be precise and ask clearly. If you're unclear of your intention, it may not turn out how you want, so be **clear**, **direct** and **concise**. Remember, **Source** is your ally and wants so much to help you, so do not be embarrassed or feel like you shouldn't be asking. It *is* what you're supposed to do. You may have been told you cannot have a direct line to Source and consequently, you've been held apart from this knowledge, and from this divine union. Through these meditations, you will see the beauty of your relationship with Source blossom and transform into something you could never have imagined possible had you stayed small, separate and disconnected, too afraid to ever ask for what you need.

Meditation Process—Connecting to Source
- ❊ Close your eyes and take three deep breaths—inhale for three counts and exhale for four counts.
- ❊ Visualise your heart space and focus in on it.
- ❊ Imagine seeing a white light beginning to glow from

the heart space. Watch it expand to fill your chest cavity, then watch it fill your whole body: from your head right down to the tips of your toes.

* Watch the light extend out of your feet and reach down into the earth. Think of it as roots growing down deep into the earth so it anchors you in. This is known as earthing to ground you.
* Once you are connected, scan up the body to the top of your head.
* From here, imagine yourself coming out of the top of your Crown Chakra (top of your head). Feel yourself fully emerge out of your physical body and become an ethereal, light spirit-body.
* Feel yourself expand so you are big.
* If you like to envision you have wings, imagine unfurling them and stretching them out so you feel completely extended and free.
* Sit with this feeling for a little while and enjoy it.
* Imagine you are shooting up as high as you can, out of the Earth's atmosphere.
* You will experience being surrounded by infinite space or light. Feel into this expansiveness.
* Imagine that this expansiveness is divine—Source/God/Universe.

NOTE: As mentioned earlier, please establish what term you are going to use as your reference—either Source, God, Universe, the All, or another chosen term/entity—and stick to it for all the meditations.

* Take notice of how the space or light shifts and morphs.

- ❈ Take notice of how you feel connecting to this.
- ❈ Now imagine you are connecting into that divinity.
- ❈ When you feel connected, acknowledge this divine being as the Creator and Source of All. Acknowledge that you are a part of that; you are a fractal of that divinity.

Allow yourself to stay with this unity for a little while and enjoy it. Remember, you are meeting **Source**. This is a sacred contact space. When you connect directly and intentionally with Source, you are entering and activating the Theta state. We are creating a portal between the physical realm and the spiritual realm.

We always connect to Source at the beginning of our session and disconnect from Source when we have completed it. We always start and end with Source.

From here, greet Source before asking what you want:

"Dear Source, Divine Creator, I ask that..."

Ask for what you want done. You are direct with your intention and with the asking. For example, let's say you're going to do a **Body Scan**. Following the greeting you'll continue:

"...a Body Scan be done. Thank you. It is done. It is complete."

Proceed with the Body Scan:

"Dear Source, Divine Creator, I ask that (for example), a Body Scan be done. Thank you. It is done. It is complete."

When you have finished your work for the session, return your attention back up to Source and ask to be disconnected in order to rejoin your body. As you separate from Source and return to your body, say **thank you** and ask to disconnect.

Meditation Process—Disconnecting from Source

- ✻ Imagine your spirit-body releasing from Source, and as it's returning to your body, you're being rinsed off in a crystalline shower or waterfall.
- ✻ Imagine yourself entering your body through the Crown Chakra, immediately going back to your Heart space.
- ✻ Once you are connected to your heart, ask for the roots connecting you to the Earth to withdraw, like you're pulling up anchor.
- ✻ Thank the Earth for holding you safe and grounded.
- ✻ Ask for any excess energy to be sent through your feet and be earthed as you're pulling up anchor.
- ✻ Then connect into your physical body, acknowledging the physicality of it, and slowly return to the room and wake up.
- ✻ To complete the process, put your right hand over your heart and silently thank Source, your body and the Earth.
- ✻ Finally, imagine placing an invisible bubble around your body, like a kind of protective energetic barrier, before getting up and going about your day. This way, you feel completely in your body, connected to it and grounded.

This is the way I recommend ending all your sessions. Connecting and disconnecting correctly is important, bringing you back into the physical dimension safely and completely.

Exercise
- » Reflect on how connecting with Source felt for you. Write down what you experienced or saw.
- » Did you experience any difficulties or challenges doing this exercise?
- » Write down any additional reflections.

*NOTE: Practice this Step two to three times to get into the feeling of it. Record more details as you go.

Reflections:

~ STEP 2 ~
How to Do a Body Scan and Notice Where Issues Are

Most of us know when there's something wrong in our body but we may not know exactly where the issue is or what part of the body is the problem. That's why learning how to do a **Body Scan** is such a great asset in helping you locate where the trouble is.

There are two parts to this Step:
 1. How to do a Body Scan.
 2. How to see the highlighted areas requiring attention.

Part 1 - The Body Scan
This is about how you **See** (or sense) your body with your Inner Eye (Third Eye). Think imagination: you are using your imagination to view or see. When you do a Body Scan, you are looking throughout your body (from inside) to find out where the problems are. You're working your way down your body, beginning from your head and ending at your toes. You're scanning through your whole body, taking notice of where things may require your attention. Most of us have an idea of what's in our body and where the organs are. However, if you're not familiar with your anatomical organs just be generic. Do not stress if you don't know exactly what organ you have where, it'll come to you intuitively. You can consult an anatomy photo/picture afterwards to help you, if required. You do not need to be perfect. Things still work out regardless. I have tested this out, so I'm confident in saying so.

When I'm scanning, sometimes it looks like I'm using a laser of light over my body, other times I'm sensing my way through. Just allow your gaze to move around the body. You'll get faster at this with practice.

Part 2 - Seeing the Problem Areas Highlighted
When you do your Body Scan, you are going to ask for the areas that require attention, or are out of alignment, to be **highlighted**.

In asking for this, you will be paying close attention, looking for these areas to **flash up**. In my case, they show up as *red*, *heat*, or *dark/shadow* areas. For you, it may be similar or something else, so pay close attention to how your Body is going to alert you to the areas requiring attention. For the sake of this exercise, though, we will ask for the highlighted areas to appear **red**.

Meditation Part 1 - The Body Scan

For this exercise, you will just be learning how to do a Body Scan. Before you do a Body Scan, you must enter your Source-connected state.

- Revisit **Step 1**. Go up and connect to Source.
- Once you've connected to Source and made your greeting or conscious connection, you will ask that a Body Scan be done:

"Dear Source, Divine Creator, I ask that you do a Body Scan. Thank you. It is done. It is complete."

- Return through the Crown Chakra (top of your head) and start scanning your body. Proceed slowly down, looking at all your body parts—front and back.
- When you've finished your scanning exercise, return to Source and disconnect.

*NOTE: This first part is only for practice and to learn to disconnect following a meditation, otherwise you would carry on meditating to view the highlighted areas—the second part of this Step.

Exercise
- » Reflect on how you saw or experienced your body. Were you able to see your body from inside or view/scan it differently?
- » Were there any difficulties or challenges in doing this exercise?
- » Write down any additional reflections.

NOTE: Practice this step at least two to three times to get used to scanning your body.

Reflections:

Meditation Part 2 - Seeing Highlighted Areas
In this part of the meditation, when doing your Body Scan, you're asking for any areas that require your attention, or the areas that are out of alignment, to be **highlighted** for you to see them clearly. You will be seeing them as **red**, like they are alerting you. Whenever you see these areas flash up, you will take notice of them because they will be attended to in **Step 3**.

You may be surprised what parts flash up, because often they can be areas you least expected to be needing attention. So have no expectations and be open and trusting.

"Dear Source, Divine Creator, I ask that a Body Scan be done and any areas requiring my attention be highlighted in red. Thank you. It is done. It is complete."

- Return to your body and repeat the scan again, beginning from the head and working down slowly through your body.
- Take notice of the areas that highlight themselves in red.
- When you've completed your Body Scan and have taken note of where the **red highlighted** areas are, return to **Source** and disconnect as in **Step 1**.

Normally, you would proceed directly to **Step 3**, however, while you're learning you'll disconnect.

Exercise
- » What areas were highlighted for you? (1 or more?)
- » Did the highlights present themselves as red or in a different way, for example as heat, shadow or a sound?
- » Were the areas that were highlighted the ones you expected, or were there unexpected areas highlighted?
- » Were there any difficulties or challenges in doing this exercise?
- » Write down any additional reflections.

NOTE: Practice this Step two to three times to get used to seeing the highlighted areas.
**NOTE: *If you couldn't view yourself from the inside, try to view yourself from the outside, as though facing yourself, and scan your body that way. If you want to imagine you're viewing a human anatomy poster, then scan that. Not everyone is going to see their body in the same way, but trust that all ways will work, regardless. If you cannot see at all then sense where the body parts are. Your intention is what is required.*

Reflections:

~ STEP 3 ~
How to Apply the Healing Blue Light

The **blue light** is healing, calming, cooling, soothing and illuminating, countering the **red** (or heat/shadow) being emitted from your body part or organ. Think about it this way: when the body is sore, inflamed, or angry it emits heat, so the blue light effectively cools the area down.

Now that we've completed our scan and we've noticed the areas requiring attention, we return to Source to apply the blue light to the affected area or areas.

Meditation Process—Blue Light Application

✺ Begin by connecting back to Source. Then ask:

"Dear Source, Divine Creator, I ask that the healing blue light be applied to (enter body part here). Thank you. It is done. It is complete."

✺ Return to your body part or organ and visualise applying the cooling calming **blue light** to the affected area.
✺ Watch as the **red** dissolves and your body part is no longer hot, inflamed, or angry.
✺ Stay with it 'til the body part responds. Take notice.
✺ Continue if you have more than one body part to attend to.
✺ When you have finished applying the blue light and witnessed this take place, return your attention back to Source and ask to be disconnected so you may rejoin your body.
✺ Upon disconnecting, ask for a cleansing.

- ✸ Imagine your spirit body being rinsed off in a crystalline shower or waterfall as you are coming back into your body through the Crown Chakra.
- ✸ Once you are cleansed and returned, immediately connect back to your Heart space.
- ✸ Once connected to your heart, ask for the roots connecting you to the Earth to withdraw anchor.
- ✸ Thank the Earth for holding you safe and grounded.
- ✸ Ask for any excess energy to be sent through your feet and earthed as you're withdrawing your roots or "pulling up anchor".
- ✸ Connect into your body, acknowledging the physicality of it, and slowly return to the room and wake up.
- ✸ Place your hand over your heart in thanks.
- ✸ Place an energetic bubble around your body to complete the meditation.

This disconnecting is exactly as in **Step 1**. We always disconnect in the same way each time we complete our work. The only time we may not disconnect properly is if we are doing this work in bed prior to sleeping, or we fall asleep during/following the healing process. This is perfectly fine as the body will continue the healing while you sleep, so do not worry about disconnecting. I do try to be conscious of closing off, though, especially if I'm going out into the world after I've done some healing work or there are others in my space needing my attention. It is always best to finish off so that you are contained and complete.

Exercise
- » How did the **blue light** application feel?
- » How did the area you were using the blue light on respond?
- » Compare before using the blue light to after using it. What changes did you notice?
- » Did you have any difficulties or challenges doing this exercise?
- » Write down any additional reflections.

NOTE: Practice at least two to three times to get used to the application of blue light AND noticing the changes.

Reflections:

~ STEP 4 ~
How to Listen to and Decipher the Messages Your Body is Revealing to You

Your body is a messenger. It is trying to get your attention in the only way it knows how—through pain, illness, disease, discomfort, and so forth—which is often to do with something emotional that is not being addressed or is being suppressed, like anger or resentment. These carry such a dense energy that they are stored up in the body, turning themselves into something far more serious if the initial emotion is not addressed and released. For example, I believe cancer is anger held onto and suppressed.

Alternatively, it may be a message to signify that you are not moving forward, or you are stagnating in life. It may be that a relationship in your life is becoming toxic, hence the body may translate this literally as a toxic situation in your body. If you are not doing what you can to address problems in your life, they will manifest into something more tangible, showing up as issues in your physical body. Your body is literally signalling to you that something is wrong, and you **MUST** pay attention, or it'll only get worse.

Understanding the Message
This next step is learning how to listen and understand what your body/body part is trying to tell you. What does it want you to know? What does it want you to do to work through or action this message and heal it? The process will be to firstly ask your body/part what it is trying to tell you, then to secondly ask how you can action it for it to heal.

It is recommended to do this Step on its own. However, once you're more proficient and practiced, you can continue from **Step 3** after applying the blue light.

Meditation Process for Understanding the Message

- Firstly, connect to Source as in Step 1. Then ask:

"Dear Source, Divine Creator, I ask what is the message my *(enter body part here)* is trying to send me? Is there anything I need to do? Thank you. It is done. It is complete."

- Return to your body part and focus on it.
- Assure your body or body part that you are listening and ready to receive the message. (You are in dialogue with your body.) Now ask:

"What is happening? What do you wish me to understand?"

- Listen to the message and then ask:

"What do I need to action or how do I work through this?

- Listen to the direction suggested and then ask:

"If I do this, will it be released?"

- Listen to the outcome.
- Tell your body or body part that the message has been received with thanks.
- When complete, return to Source to disconnect as in **Step 1.**

**NOTE: If you can perform the required action during the healing session, then proceed. If it is something that is required outside of the session, for example ending a relationship or leaving a job, then you will do this in optimum timing for the healing to be completed. If it was something like, "You need to love yourself," then you can start this in the session and continue outside of the session. Carry on with the next Steps because they will continue to support and assist your healing.*

Exercise
- » What is the message revealed to you from this body part and how was the message relayed to you? It could be with words, in visuals, with feelings or emotions, as sounds, or something else.
- » What is the action required or what does the body part want you to do, and can you do so in the session?
- » If you action the message, how long will it take to heal or release this issue?
- » Are you feeling any resistance or blocks around the message and what it's asking of you?
- » Did you experience any difficulties or challenges doing this exercise?
- » Write down any additional reflections.

NOTE: Practice at least two to three times to get used to how your body is going to relay its messages to you. It may be in several ways.
**NOTE: Do this step for each highlighted area individually. Process/reflect on each one separately too.*

Reflections:

Before we move onto **Step 5**, I want to share a personal anecdote here because I feel it'll give you insight into the process.

A few weeks ago, I woke to find my left thumb was hurting me. The joint was inflamed and I could barely bend it. It felt arthritic. I wondered if I'd done something to hurt it, but I couldn't recall anything. For a couple of days, I just looked out for it, trying not to do anything that might further aggravate it. I tried essential oils, heating it and cooling it, but nothing really worked. After a few days, it was getting worse, so I decided it was time to look in and ask what was happening to it.

I connected to **Source** and asked for the application of the **blue light** to reduce the inflammation. I asked what was happening to my thumb to find out what the message was. As soon as I connected into my thumb, it immediately revealed the **message**. When I was five-years-old, my thumb was broken by someone in my family. This was a traumatic childhood event I thought I'd healed. However, it was obvious that my thumb was still carrying some residual trauma that had been triggered a few days before. The trigger was a Quantum Healing client who'd come to heal both her hands, including her thumbs. Rarely am I triggered by my clients, but even though *I* had not remembered any connection to my past, my thumb had.

It was fascinating to me that although I felt detached from that incident, my thumb had not let it go fully. So, I apologised to my thumb for what it was experiencing, and I said that I was okay and would do more healing around that event. What I was required to do (the **action**) was forgive the event and the person involved. I completed **Step 9 Forgiveness Work** and then disconnected from **Source**, returning to my body and finalising my session.

I made sure that for the rest of the day I did not use my hand much, treating it as if it had just been bandaged up in surgery and it was mending itself. By the end of the day, it was feeling so much better; the swelling had gone down and I could bend it a little. When I awoke the next day, it was about 95% recovered and within a couple of days, it was almost completely recovered. No more inflammation, no more pain and no arthritic evidence was there. It does get a little stiff occasionally, but other than that it is healed.

The **message** was acknowledged, the **action** was taken, and the healing was completed with the trauma being **released** along with the past. And that's how it's done.

~ STEP 5 ~
Identifying Your Limiting Belief Systems and Replacing Them

I spoke of limiting belief systems earlier in *Self-Commitment No. 3* and how they impact us without our awareness. This next Step will help you find out what your limiting beliefs or belief systems are, then help you to replace them with those that are positive, support wellness and wellbeing, and help you live your best life.

Think about what limiting beliefs you have around your illness or your life. I want you to dig deep and be honest with yourself. If you need to meditate on it, do so. Sometimes you'll begin with one belief but continue digging deeper 'til you find the **bottom-line** belief that forms the basis for all things. It could be beliefs like, "I do not deserve to be here" **or**, "I am unlovable" **or**, "I am not worthy of living or being well". There is always the one that sits right underneath everything, dictating your life and holding you apart from your fullest potential to heal. This is the one we want to remove, resolve, dissolve and replace!

Exercise
- » Can you identify any limiting beliefs you have around healing? For example, "I don't believe I can heal" or, "I have this illness because my mother had it".
- » Can you identify any limiting beliefs you have in your life at all? For example, "I believe as we age, we get sicker" or, "I am not worthy of love".

Take a quiet moment to think of any beliefs that come up. Keep digging under them 'til you get to a core belief (ones about ourselves, other people, and our world) . Write it down because you will use it in the meditation exercise.

Limiting Beliefs:

~~~~~~

~~~~~~

~~~~~~

~~~~~~

~~~~~~

~~~~~~

~~~~~~

~~~~~~

If you are struggling, you can go into meditation and apply the same process you did for the previous **Step** and ask directly from that body part, or from yourself:

"What limiting beliefs do I have that present an obstacle to my healing?"

Then return and write it/them down.

Secondly, you need to find a replacement belief. Because you are going to 'swap out' the old belief for this new belief, it needs to be one that you will love having as your replacement. It needs to be one that truly resonates with you, and that feels natural and comfortable. It may not always be the direct opposite of the limiting belief, so I want you to keep considering different alternatives 'til you find the one that fits most perfectly. When you speak it out loud, you feel good saying it, and it sits comfortably with you.

Exercise
Now you've identified the limiting beliefs, what do you wish to replace them with? Some examples are, "I believe I CAN heal" or even better, "I AM HEALED!" or, "I am free from carrying this genetic/ancestral illness forward".

» Write down what you would like to replace your limiting belief with. Remember, it is always 'a positive', so think of phrases such as positive affirmations.

Replacement Beliefs:

~~~~~~

~~~~~~

~~~~~~

~~~~~~

~~~~~~

~~~~~~

~~~~~~

~~~~~~

Now you have identified the belief, that needs replacing and the belief you are replacing it with, you can proceed to the **meditation**.

Meditation Process–Removing a Limiting Belief and Replacing It
- ❋ Firstly, connect to Source as in **Step 1**.
- ❋ Ask Source for the limiting belief you've identified to be retrieved, cleared and replaced.

"Dear Source, Divine Creator, I ask that the limiting belief *(insert belief here)* be retrieved, cleared, and replaced with the new belief *(enter new belief here)*. Thank you. It is done. It is complete."

- ❋ Return to your body and focus on your mind.
- ❋ Ask for the **belief** to reveal itself.
- ❋ Imagine it appearing like a document with the belief written on it.
- ❋ Ask for the belief to be cleared and resolved.
- ❋ Witness it being sent up to Source to be cleared and resolved in light.
- ❋ Now focus your attention on your **new belief** (the one you have chosen to replace the old one with).
- ❋ Imagine it as a shining new document, signed by Source with a gold seal on it.
- ❋ Witness it being replaced in your mind.
- ❋ Now go back up to Source and disconnect (**Step 1**).

NOTE: If you identified any beliefs that are ancestral or genetic you may wish to continue to work on that in Step 6 after completing this step.

Exercise
- » How did the original belief reveal itself?
- » How did you remove it or destroy it?
- » What did your new replacement belief look like?
- » Was it easy to swap them out?
- » How does it feel now that you have replaced your belief with a brand new one?
- » Did you experience any difficulties or challenges doing this exercise?
- » Write down all you experienced here, especially any emotional releases or further insights you may have had. Add any additional reflections.

*NOTE: Practice at least two to three times to get used to this process. Do this step for each limiting belief. Process/reflect on each one separately too.

Reflections:

Before we continue to **Step 6**, I'd like to share an anecdote of a client whose limiting belief was holding her apart from living her life. We began by trying to uncover why she was exhausting herself doing everything for her family and feeling so guilty when she gave to herself. As we dug in, we discovered my client's belief was, "It's my duty to do everything for everyone." In her mind, it was her duty to look after everyone at the expense of herself; she believed it was what women did. It was certainly what her mother did, putting everyone else first at her own expense. She was conditioned to believe that being a good mother meant sacrificing yourself because it was your duty to do so. This was an ancestral belief that had been handed down.

As we discussed what she'd like to replace the belief with, she found that her new belief was, "I have the **free will** to choose for myself." She was no longer obligated to everyone else at the expense of herself, and she had the right to choose what was right for her. She could give without it being at the expense of herself. This new belief felt right for her. It felt organic and comfortable as a replacement, and it made her feel self-empowered.

The clearing process was activated (as in the meditation) to ensure the old belief was removed, cleared and resolved. Then the new belief contract was installed and filed away, leaving her feeling like she was worthy and deserving.

~ STEP 6 ~
Identifying Ancestral Beliefs, Illnesses and Programs and Clearing Them

Think about the genetic illnesses that you take for granted as part of your genetic make-up; those you believe may manifest at some point, if they haven't already. It can be anything from cancer to arthritis, or it can be something you were born with. The illnesses you were born with tend to be contracted for this lifetime, in other words you chose to experience it as a way to learn from it. Then, there are those that occur later in life; these are the ones you worry about becoming active. For example, women believe they are more likely to get breast cancer if their mother had it. Some will even take preventative measures and have mastectomies to avoid this occurring. Whilst I don't judge people for doing this, if they understood how they are in charge of their body and its experience, they could alter the course of their destiny because, essentially, that's what they are believing—that they are destined to have the same condition their mother had. It would certainly reduce their worrying and perhaps even the premature mastectomies. However, I am not a doctor, so it is not my place to decide for anyone what feels right for them.

But I would like you to consider the alternative and prevent any unnecessary trauma to your body, because surgery is essentially trauma even if it is advised. When you understand the metaphysical process of healing, you will learn that you can activate or deactivate illnesses that are genetic. In essence, you do *not* have to experience breast cancer just because your mother did. You can effectively heal your ancestral illnesses and even alter your **DNA** (coming up in **Step 7**). You are not locked into your ancestral destiny.

Emotional ancestral baggage may also carry over and manifest in your life as a physical illness. For instance, women in your family line may never have had a voice and as this tends to carry over in conditioning and beliefs. It can manifest in your life as thyroid issues or Throat Chakra complications, so **speaking up** or learning to have a voice becomes the antidote.

You can see how ancestral issues can be about genetics, beliefs, and programming. Any or all of these may present themselves during your healing. It may come up as something relative to your illness, directly or indirectly, by keeping you in suffering or limitation. Whatever is presented, work through it as this is essential to healing not just your physical body but your emotional, psychological and spiritual body too. Remember, you are multi-layered and multi-dimensional, so you must work in the same way.

NOTE: This meditation step can be intricate as you may identify several ancestral issues that require healing. Each one will therefore need to be attended to individually.

There are two meditation processes: one for those who do *not* know what their ancestral issues are, and another for those who *do* know what they are.

If you do know what you wish to heal, skip the next meditation and go directly to **Meditation Process—Clearing Ancestral Issues**.

Meditation Process—Identify ancestral issues
- ❋ Connect to Source with **Step 1**. Then ask:

"Dear Source, Divine Creator, I ask you to identify what ancestral beliefs or issues I'm carrying and how it relates to my illness."

- ❋ You can either return to the body and go to the site of the illness or sit with Source to receive the answer.
- ❋ When you receive the answer, disconnect from Source and complete the exercise.

Exercise
- » What ancestral genetic issues have you identified ? Write these down.
- » What ancestral beliefs have you identified? Write these down.

NOTE: If you've identified more than one genetic ancestral issue or belief, you'll attend to each one separately in the meditation.

Reflections:

If you **do** know what you wish to clear:
Exercise
- » What ancestral genetic issues do you know about? Write these down.
- » What ancestral beliefs do you know you hold? Write these down.

NOTE: If you could not identify one or both of these, then ask Source in the meditation.

Reflections:

~~~~~~

~~~~~~

~~~~~~

~~~~~~

~~~~~~

~~~~~~

~~~~~~

~~~~~~

Once you've identified physical ancestral genetic issues and/or ancestral beliefs (that is, intergenerational emotional issues), you'll now attend to each one separately in the following meditation.

Meditation Process–Clearing Ancestral Issues

❋ Connect to Source with Step 1. Then ask:

"Dear Source, Divine Creator, I ask for this *(enter genetic issue/belief)* to be cleared and healed all the way back into the past for all my ancestors, into the present, and going forward into the future for all forthcoming generations. Thank you. It is done. It is complete."

❋ Return to your body to witness these ancestral issues/beliefs being extracted from you and being sent up to Source to be healed and cleared. We are saying goodbye to old patterns, programs, stories, and/or illnesses. We are acknowledging that they no longer exist in the present, nor will carry forward into the future.

❋ If you are healing a physical manifestation of it, then please witness this clearing and healing too. Witness it being healed in the present and going forward into the future.

❋ Finalise your session by disconnecting (as in **Step 1**) when you have completed this process.

NOTE: Repeat this process for each issue individually.

Exercise
- » What did you experience or witness during this meditation of healing ancestral and/or genetic issues?
- » How did the healing take place? What did you notice?
- » How do you feel after this exercise?
- » Did you experience any difficulties or challenges doing this exercise?
- » Write down any additional reflections.

Reflections:

_____

_____

_____

_____

_____

_____

_____

_____

*NOTE: Practice at least two to three times to get used to this process.

For more work on our genetics, we will proceed to **Step 7** and **Step 8**, working on our DNA. This will complete all our physical work.

~ STEP 7 ~
How to Communicate With Your DNA and Switch ON/OFF Genetic Markers

The first time I ever worked with my DNA was during my ThetaHealing® training. It was incredible that I was able to view and talk directly to my DNA, the very thing that made ME. I not only saw my DNA strands but the genetic markers that were carrying undesirable traits and learned I had the power to switch them OFF (or ON as applicable) so they were no longer a threat.

It was many years later that I stumbled across a journal article about a science called Epigenetics. It was in reference to Russian scientists, their studies around DNA and how we and our environment can *affect* our DNA. Upon researching a little more, it seemed Epigenetics had roots stemming back to 1927 Russia. It was considered quite controversial by Western Science, yet in recent years, according to Graham (2016), this field in biology had boomed across the globe. [10] Graham also said that environmental influences can cause changes to the genes, which can be turned ON or OFF or, in other words, the genes can be expressed or not expressed. To me, this is a clear indication that there is a science correlating to what I am speaking about here in spiritual and metaphysical terms.

As I like to say, science is only just catching up with ancient knowledge and Source's wisdom. They're the things we have innately known as a species for many eons, prior to science pitching itself forward in the last couple of hundred years; the *only* legitimate source of knowledge with regards to healing. If you wish to read about ancient healing and science's encroachment on traditional healing (using it, but not acknowledging its use), there are many books written on this subject.

---

10 GRAHAM, L. (2016). Epigenetics and Russia. Proceedings of the American Philosophical Society, 160(3), 266-271. http://www.jstor.org/stable/26159182

Ironically, science has drawn on old methods and practices of traditional and herbal healing, including the medicinal aspects, yet continues to disregard or offer recognition of their legitimacy. There are books written by scientists who *do* acknowledge the existence and legitimacy of traditional methods of healing and herbal remedies, giving them more credibility. In a way, it offers humanity permission to open up to alternative and holistic healing if it's endorsed or recommended by a scientist. That's a positive, however, I say give credit where credit's due! For some of you, reading this book and learning the meditations may be all that is required to feel confident and courageous enough to trust your own body's innate ability to heal, with the divine intervention and assistance of **Source**. At the end of the day, Source is always there, no matter with which method you choose to heal. You have a direct line.

The whole idea of talking to your DNA is quite fascinating and it's still a wonder to me that we can, but once you understand that your body is a communicative living universe, then it's no surprise. I have worked on my DNA many times in my life and, of course, the last time was in 2019 to clear the undesirable illnesses that were flashing up in my system. These were: Lupus, Sjogren's, Arthritis and Rheumatoid Arthritis. The last two were considered hereditary and identified as being active when I was initially tested for the **mystery illness**. However, they never showed up again or were inconclusive once I'd begun healing myself.

Our DNA is currently a double helix, meaning two strands that intertwine. However, as our species is evolving, it will become a 12-Stranded DNA. According to Source, this is our original blueprint DNA structure, by Divine Instruction, but ten of our strands remain dormant due to them being **asleep**. We ourselves, as a human race, have been asleep, slumbering in the matrix of the very basic living requirements. We've lost our abilities to be expansive, telepathic, psychic and multi/inter-dimensional. We've deliberately been separated from our **divine essence**, our direct line to **Source** severed. We've fallen asleep and lost all trace of our divinity.

Now, as we are at the apex of our evolution, finally we're awakening to our own true nature and, as such, our bodies are responding to this. They're going through remarkable changes, returning to their biological blueprint, crystalline structures that include the activation of the 12-Strand DNA. Initially, when I trained as a ThetaHealer® in the early 2000s, we would consciously activate these 12-Strands. Now, according to many QHHT® clients, our DNA is undergoing this transformation by itself, assisted by a shift in the collective consciousness and our realisation of our divinity.

This is such exciting news. This means no more illness, no more aging, no more disruption or interference in our body matrix. Our future selves will be free from all the corruptions our current bodies are dealing with but, for now, whilst we are currently in a double helix DNA format, we will learn to work with them as they are. I will not be outlining the 12-Strand DNA activation process in this book because this is part of the ThetaHealing® modality.

When you view your own DNA for the first time, they may not seem as bright and bubbly, **standing-to-attention**, little soldiers as they should be. They can appear inactive, slow, sad, sluggish, drab-looking, or even fuzzy, because they have not been attended to for a long time. What we are going to do is bring them back into alignment before we do any work on them, so that they are spritely and attentive.

There are 2 parts to this exercise:
1. Viewing DNA and activating the white light.
2. Viewing DNA markers and switching them OFF.

For the first part of this exercise, you will be viewing your 46 DNA strands in their 23 chromosomal pairs (two DNA strands equates to one chromosomal pair.) To do this, you will firstly access the pineal gland located in the centre of your brain. Within this gland is the Master Cell— the very first cell all others in your body are replicated from. Within this Master Cell is the Master Nucleus, housing the Master DNA coding for you. Within there resides the 23 pairs of chromosomes, including the sex chromosomes: XX (female) or XY (male). Each pair will be unique in appearance and size and consist of two similar looking double helix strands. They'll range from teeny tiny and squat looking to quite large and slim, all in random order. The idea is to look at them or sense them and to take notice of how they appear; whether they're looking droopy or bright? You'll then be sending in **white light** to activate them and bring them back *online* again.

Meditation Process Part 1–DNA Viewing and White Light Activation

- ❋ Connect to Source with Step 1.

NOTE: You are not going to ask for anything at this stage.

- ❋ Return to the body via Crown.
- ❋ Imagine accessing your pineal gland (centre brain). Travel inside this and view the **Master Cell**.
- ❋ Once in the Master Cell, travel inside and locate the **Master Nucleus**, which contains your **Master DNA**.
- ❋ Imagine seeing your DNA (in their chromosomal pairs) lined up in a row.
- ❋ Scan them, one pair at a time, taking notice of how they look and whether any are sluggish or spritely.
- ❋ Once you've scanned them, you will return to Source to ask for an activation using the healing **white light**.

"Dear Source, Divine Creator, I ask that my DNA be activated with the healing white light. Thank you. It is done. It is complete."

- ❋ Return to your pineal gland, going into the Master Cell, to the Master Nucleus to view the chromosomal pairs of DNA strands within.
- ❋ Witness each pair, one at a time, being activated by applying the healing **white light**.

NOTE: Pay attention to the ones needing a little more care as you go. Some do require a little more healing.

- ❋ Once you've **white light**-ed each pair, return to **Source** and disconnect to complete the session.

Exercise
- » Were you able to visualise your DNA (chromosomal pairs) and if so, how did your DNA look to you when you first saw them?
- » How did your DNA look and/or feel after applying the **white light**? Was there a difference?
- » Did you experience any difficulties or challenges doing this exercise?
- » Write down any additional reflections.

Reflections:

~~~~~~

~~~~~~

~~~~~~

~~~~~~

~~~~~~

~~~~~~

~~~~~~

~~~~~~

*NOTE: Practice at least two to three times to get used to seeing your DNA and using the white light process.

The second part of this exercise is to do with the markers on the strands. Markers are tiny, coded blocks of information carried on the DNA strands. There are literally thousands of these markers carrying instructions that make YOU who you are. They are random combinations of both of your parents' DNA, carried down ancestrally. Occasionally, those markers carry genetic illnesses, which are carried forward through your lineage, but it is important to note that they are *not* always switched ON or activated by default. This is not information science knows about (or if so, only in recent years) and it may even counter scientific community knowledge. But having done this healing work for over 20 years, I have learned that these markers are flexible and responsive to their environment, your beliefs and requests. They are not dumb, stagnant things but active, alive, adaptable beings. When you're doing DNA work for your genetic illnesses or diseases, it's important to check if any of the markers associated with these are actually switched ON and if they are you'll switch them OFF.

For this meditation exercise you're going to scan your DNA again, as you did in the previous meditation exercise. However, this time you're going to ask for the **markers** relating to the genetic illnesses (whether the illness is dormant or not) to reveal themselves so you can *see* (or sense) them. Once they reveal themselves to you, I want you to thank them for doing a wonderful job. Remember they are not doing anything wrong; they are only carrying out the instructions given to them (by your ancestors or you/your beliefs) to be active. So, you are thanking them for doing their job, thanking them for the lessons you have learnt from the experience, and letting them know they are no longer required to be active; they can switch OFF.

You will then ask them to return to their original *Divine Blueprint* that **Source** intended for them, aligned with wellness and wellbeing. You are asking Source therefore to switch OFF the markers and return them to their original *Divine Blueprint* and reactivate the *Wellness Codes*—**The God Codes** (coded messages within the molecules of life, deep within the DNA in each cell of our bodies).

Meditation Process Part 2–Viewing DNA Markers and Switching Them OFF

❋ Connect to Source with Step 1. Then ask:

"Dear Source, Divine Creator, I ask for any markers relating to my illness *(insert either symptoms or diagnoses here)* to be revealed so that they may be switched OFF. I ask that the *Wellness Codes* be switched ON in their place so that all is aligned with the original *Divine Blueprint* as was originally intended. Thank you. It is done. It is complete."

❋ Enter the pineal gland, the Master Cell, the Master Nucleus, and focus on the Master DNA
❋ Scan your chromosomal pairs as you did in the previous exercise, but this time you are looking for the **markers** to reveal themselves. They are going to reveal themselves uniquely to you, perhaps as a fluorescent yellow colour or as dark patches, so pay attention. Remember, it is okay to **sense** them if you can't see them.
❋ Thank them for their efforts and ask them to switch OFF.
❋ Watch this happen.
❋ Ask for them to return to the original Divine Blueprint.
❋ Ask for the *Wellness Codes* to be activated.
❋ Watch as this process takes place.

NOTE: Witnessing the event is actualising it! You must witness it for it to become actualised in the Third Dimension.

❋ Once you've finished, return to Source to disconnect.

In **Step 8**, you are asking for this action to be replicated throughout every cell in your body.

Exercise
- » Were you able to see the markers highlighted? How did they reveal themselves to you?
- » How did they appear once you switched them OFF and activated the *Wellness Codes*?
- » How do you feel after this exercise?
- » Did you experience any difficulties or challenges doing this exercise?
- » Write down any additional reflections.

NOTE: Practice at least two to three times to get used to this process.

Reflections:

~ STEP 8 ~
Communicating With the Cells in Your Body

There are approximately one hundred trillion cells in your body. Imagine each cell must have this new information installed as an upgrade, like a computer having new software installed for the system to be upgraded. For this to occur in the body, each cell needs to receive the information via communication. It is like a network, each cell receiving the information, communicating it on to the next cell, and so on 'til it reaches every single cell in the body. This process requires the cells of the body to act as a united community. It is asking every cell to be aware, awake and participate in your **body universe** to distribute this new information. We are therefore asking our cells to unite and become one.

In many instances, our cells are not really aware of each other because we have not paid our body much attention, so although it functions, it is not as a united community. You are the **Supreme Being** in charge of your **body universe**. It *will* respond to whatever you ask of it. Whatever you tell it (whether that's telling it that it's wonderful or it's horrible), it *will* obey. You must therefore be forever vigilant and mindful of what you're instructing your body to do. You are responsible for its program activation!

For this next meditation, you're going to ask that the new information (the DNA upgrade from the previous exercise) be shared with each cell in your body. Of course, you can't watch it go from cell to cell or you'd be there forever, so simply imagine this information spreading like an energy field throughout your body. Witness it as a light coursing through and around your body. It is going to take a little time to reach every cell, but as you have already *seen* it take place in the astral, trust it is done and completed and will manifest very soon in the Third Dimension.

You're also asking your cells to unite as a community, rallying for you to be well, so talk to them and encourage them to get on board together for a common cause. Ask them to become allies to support you in this process and to spread the word.

In practice, once you know how this process works, you can continue directly onto this stage after activating the DNA upgrades. For this exercise, however, you will do this as a separate meditation.

Meditation Process–Communicating Upgrades With Your Cells

❋ Connect to Source with **Step 1**. Then ask:

"Dear Source, Divine Creator, I ask that the DNA work I just completed in my Master Cell be replicated throughout every single cell in my body. Let every cell switch OFF the relevant markers and activate the Wellness Codes. Thank you. It is done. It is complete."

❋ Return to the Master Cell and ask it to share the information with all the cells in your body.
❋ Witness this information spreading throughout your body like a network.
❋ When you've completed this, disconnect from Source to complete your process.

*NOTE: I suggest remaining in a meditative state for a while or even go to sleep to allow your body to spread the message without being disrupted. I personally do this work before I go to sleep at night so it can be completed during my sleep state.

Exercise
- » What was it like to connect with your cells? Were they able to connect as a community?
- » How were the messages or upgrades being communicated between the cells?
- » Did you experience any difficulties or challenges doing this exercise?
- » Write down any additional reflections.

NOTE: Practice at least two to three times to get used to seeing your cells communicating together.

Reflections:

This is the completion of the Metaphysical Healing Steps. However, I believe that to heal physically we need to heal any residual emotional baggage that may become a hindrance to our complete healing process. Therefore, I've added in the final step, **Step 9**, which I believe is a must do in order to let go of all those who have wronged us or caused us pain and suffering. Why? Because we carry the trauma, not them, and it festers in our body causing us unwellness and illness. So best to release it once and for all now that we've come so far in our healing process.

For this, we will proceed to **Step 9 Forgiveness Work.**

~ STEP 9 ~
Forgiveness Work

I spent years trying to understand what forgiveness was. I always thought that to forgive someone for the wrongs they had committed against me was somehow letting them get away with what they'd done. It also meant that when I forgave them, I would also be letting go of the trauma and hurt associated with them, yet I struggled to see how I could let them get away with it and, simultaneously, let go of an integral part of my identity. I was so attached to my trauma and wounding that I didn't know who I was without it—my trauma defined *who* I was. I thought that if I let my traumas and the stories associated with them go, then who would know my story? It felt like letting the story go meant there would no longer be anyone there to bear witness to my trauma, or to legitimise my suffering. I could not understand how forgiveness benefitted me, when all I could see was that it benefitted the others and then erased my story and, in turn, me.

I consulted so many books on it and couldn't find anything that resonated with me or comforted me. It was like every writer or speaker on the topic just assumed you knew what it was, what it meant and how to do it, yet no one actually explained the process. It was all so abstract and intangible. Then one day, while I was scrolling social media, I came across a short video made by a female reverend speaking on the topic of forgiveness. She spoke of how the burden the sufferer carried was so enormous that it robbed the sufferer from living. The victim was the only one suffering and no one else was. Carrying around the responsibility of that hurt and pain was actually killing the very person who wished to be free of it. The victim was continually suffering because the load was far too heavy to carry year after year.

What I understood from this was that essentially, the sufferer is missing out on living this life fully and deserved to be free from carrying the burden in order to be lighter and live. But in order to release the weight of the burden, they had to **forgive**. By doing so, they were essentially sending back that load to the person responsible for creating it in the first place, and by this act, they were dissolving the hurt, the person, the situation completely from their lives, their memories, and their past. Through the act of **forgiveness**, we let all of it go to be resolved, dissolved and healed from our core selves, thus freeing us up from carrying that burden any longer.

What she said resonated with me, yet I still didn't know exactly how to do it. How could I *action* this forgiveness in a way that didn't require me to confront that person and do it personally? It would take a little while longer 'til the answer arrived. When I connected to **Source** through my healing and spiritual work, I asked the question, 'How do I action forgiveness?' and the answer was eventually delivered in a format that I could understand. In this instance, it manifested in one of Dolores Cannon's books I was reading.

Dolores was probably the most influential in my understanding of forgiveness and how to action it. She reiterated what I'd heard in the reverend's video but went on to explain *how* to do it. She made it all so simple and easy, and it has continued to be an integral part of my ongoing spiritual practice. So, to complete the **Forgiveness Work** step, I have decided to use a variation of her wording because I think it's the easiest and most non-threatening way to action forgiveness.

There are two ways to do the Forgiveness Work:
1. **If you already know who you wish to forgive**
    - Identify any person/s or situation/s you'd like to do forgiveness work for and write them down.
    - Proceed directly to **Meditation Process Part 2–Continue With Forgiveness Work.**

2. **If you do not know who you wish to forgive**
    - Connect to Source and ask what, or who, is requiring forgiveness in association with your illness or body/part.

Meditation Process Part 1—Finding Out Who to Forgive

❋ Connect to Source with Step 1. Ask:

"Dearest Source, Divine Creator, I ask you to show me what in my life needs forgiveness in relation to my illness (or disease/body part)? What or who is holding me apart from complete healing? Thank you. It is done. It is complete."

❋ Direct your attention to the body area or the illness and tap in to see what is revealed.

NOTE: It could be a memory or a vision of a time in your life that was difficult. Maybe a person will flash up for you. Whatever is revealed, do not dismiss it even if you feel it is minor, or that you've already dealt with it. Sometimes, it is a small thing buried deeply because it was not seen as significant enough for your attention to clear it before, or perhaps you've done a lot of work around something or someone and thought it was completed already. If it surfaces, it means there is still something residual remaining for you to finish and release completely.

❋ Once you've identified the situation, person or past that is requiring forgiveness and release, return to record what you've found. There is no need to disconnect from **Source** because you will return directly to continue after the following exercise.

Exercise
- » Who or what was revealed in relation to the body part or illness, requiring forgiveness? Write down the names or situation details.
- » Was it what you expected or was it unexpected?
- » Did you experience any difficulties or challenges doing this exercise?
- » Write down any additional reflections.

Reflections:

~~~~~~

~~~~~~

~~~~~~

~~~~~~

~~~~~~

~~~~~~

~~~~~~

Proceed with the rest of the Forgiveness meditation.

Meditation Process Part 2–Continue With Forgiveness Work
(If you already know who you need to forgive, begin here.)

You are asking for assistance to forgive those or that which you have identified in the previous exercise to be forgiven, resolved and dissolved from your past, in the present and into your future. All bonds with that time and/or that person are to be dissolved and released from you so you may be free in the present, going forward into the future.

* ❋ Return (or connect as applicable) to Source and ask:

"Dearest Source, I ask that you assist me in forgiving *(enter person or situation or time here)* and to resolve and dissolve it/them completely, so that I no longer carry this burden. I ask that it/they may be released completely from my body and soul. I also ask that all bonds be dissolved with it/them from the past, into the present and going forward into the future. Thank you. It is done. It is complete."

* ❋ Direct your attention (whilst still connected to Source) to that person or time and (*in a variation on Dolores' words*) you will say,

"I forgive you for not being what *I* wanted you to be. Forgive *me* for not being what *you* wanted me to be. We really tried but we could not make it work. I release you from me completely by breaking all bonds with you from the past, in the present and into the future. I now release you with love, so that you may go on your way, and I'll go on mine. Go with love. Be at peace."

* ❋ Watch them (if they are people) hop onto a cloud and wave them goodbye as they float away or watch them simply being sent up to **Source** to be dissolved into healing light. If it's a situation or time, just imagine healing light whirling around that time, being

dissolved as it's healed and cleared.
- ❋ Disconnect from Source, thanking them.
- ❋ Ask Source to cleanse you in a crystalline shower as you return to your body.
- ❋ Witness this.
- ❋ Once returned to your body, disconnect from the Earth, withdrawing your roots, or *pulling up anchor*, thanking Her for holding you safe and grounded during your healing.
- ❋ Return to your Heart Centre, remaining there for a minute or so to regroup.
- ❋ Bring your awareness to your physical body, then to the room and finally, when you are ready, wake up.
- ❋ Sit quietly to connect back to yourself and your surroundings.
- ❋ The Step is completed.

**NOTE: If you feel emotional during or after this Forgiveness process, please honour yourself. This is a huge step and not one to be taken lightly. It is, however, one of the easiest ways to forgive and, as a result, help you heal faster and more effectively, if not permanently. You are releasing this burden from your body and soul, your past and your future. It is a wonderful feeling to finally let go and be free.*

Exercise
- » How was this forgiveness process for you?
- » What did you notice about the person/s or situation/s you were forgiving?
- » How do you feel after completing this exercise?
- » Did you experience any difficulties or challenges doing this exercise?
- » Write down any additional reflections.

Reflections:

_____

_____

_____

_____

_____

_____

_____

NOTE: Practice at least two to three times to get used to the forgiveness process.

I wish to say, because I feel it is an important insight for you, that after completing your forgiveness work, you may still retain the memory of the episode or person you've done your forgiveness work on. However, it/they will be further away from you, or even removed from you, so they no longer have any impact upon you. In time, you will not feel the same intense emotional attachment to the experience or memory like you did before. Although it may remain as a memory, it will no longer hurt you, burden you or hold you to ransom if it flashes up; it will simply be in the past where it belongs, no longer held close by you. You will view it as an event or someone you knew in the past without bringing forward the emotional trauma or experience along with it. Essentially, you become a detached observer or witness to it.

This is how forgiveness works. It releases you from the emotional trauma and wounding. It no longer feels as though you are reliving the past (time or situation) over and over in the present. That's what happens with unresolved trauma—it remains in the present alongside you, every moment of every day. Once it is released through forgiveness, it returns to the time it existed in and it remains there, inert and harmless. It becomes a detached memory that is no longer embodied within you. What a blessing to finally be freed from that burden!

But wait! Why stop at one trauma when you can clear them all? You can repeat this process for all situations that may not have anything to do with your body or illness. You can just ask Source to assist you and proceed with the Forgiveness Work anytime, anywhere for anyone. I myself do it regularly. If I've had a current episode where someone has hurt me, I will release them from me immediately by actioning this Step. Sometimes, I release a whole group of people in one hit, putting them all on a cloud and releasing them altogether, waving them goodbye, or dissolving them in light as they are sent up to Source to deal with.

You will find this such a wonderful tool to have in your healing kit, freeing yourself anytime from any burdens, traumas or hurts. It's such a great feeling to be in charge of your own self. Remember, you get to choose what you wish to carry around while going forward on your journey from here. You are free to exist in peace. You are free to be present in the now. You are self-empowered in your knowing and how to apply it in your world, anytime. It has certainly saved me in so many ways, I hope it will save you too.

~ Conclusion ~

When I began writing this book, all I knew was that my mission was to put my self-healing knowledge onto paper for others to learn. I didn't really have a format in mind, but I knew that it needed to be written as a teaching tool for self-healing. With the assistance of a wonderful publisher who believed in me and my work (thank you, Lisa), teamed with a thorough editor, (thank you, Michelle), I was able to create a far better self-healing handbook than I could have imagined.

Telling my personal story was probably the most challenging. Not because the memories triggered me (long past that) but choosing the right parts that added value to the book without getting bogged down in the nitty-gritty of my traumas was the difficult part. However, telling something of my personal story was important to reveal the why of this healing book. Everything that I'd been through emotionally culminated in the mystery illness I had succumbed to. In order to heal my body, I had to heal all parts of myself. With Divine Instruction, self-love and forgiveness, I was finally able to accomplish this, then go on and live the life I was meant to: becoming the spiritual healer, educator and author I am today.

As we come to the end of this book, our journey together is complete. All the processes and procedures for your self-healing protocol have been clearly laid out for you to activate. From the importance of self-healing (how it benefits your wellbeing and how to set up a supportive environment), to how to conduct your self-healing (using the meditations along with the exercises) has been created to make self-healing easy for you to do. All the elements are there for you to work through in your own way, in your own time. Practice them 'til you integrate them into your being.

Remember, there is no have to or should when it comes to healing your body or yourself—you're allowed to be flexible with it and adapt it to your needs. The only process I would not recommend adapting or leaving out is Step 1. Connecting to Source. You need Source's assistance and guidance because you are the vehicle for Source's Divine Healing to travel through, and you are in communion with The Divine. It doesn't get any greater or more expansive than that.

You will heal if it is what your heart truly desires. You will heal if you put your mind to it. You have the power. Be kind to yourself, praise yourself always, and remember to always have hope. It is hope and a positive mindset that keeps us forever moving forward in our journey in this life. We can only ever be so certain of ourselves in the present moment. Whatever is on the horizon is not ours to know because it only worries us and creates more uncertainty. By remaining grounded in the present, we only have to deal with now, today. That is the only thing you have control over—you, today.

As for healing yourselves, it's one little step at a time. Do not look at the future or give yourself a deadline but stay present and focused on here and now. Heal the past because this keeps you trapped there and release the need to know what your destiny in the future is because it steals your attention away from your body. Your body needs you to be present when it's healing. It wants to know you are there for it. So, step away from the edge of uncertainty and the abyss of despair and be here now.

It is your story that gets told of whether you survive or thrive and you get to tell it how you want it to be. That's what I did. I told the story of how I believed it to be. I said, "That is not my story. It's not how my story goes." And off I went surrendering myself to Source, knowing that I had this and Source had me.

You've got this. I believe in you.

For those wondering about the elephant in the room—What happens if I die after all the healing I've done?—this is what I say to you: if your spirit has chosen to exit this Third Dimensional Earth plane of existence and transition to the light, then that is part of the grand plan that you really have no control over. In fact, you have contracted for this to occur, so nothing is ever unexpected or an accident. The reality is you will depart at some point, that is a given, but you are still living right up to that point. Whether it's now or later, or due to an illness or not, the best you can do is live the best way you know how.

Healing your spirit before you transition out of the physical realm is still worthwhile doing. Nothing is ever a wasted effort. No amount of healing the self is worthless. If anything, it will assist the easing of your spirit as it lets go of the physical and embraces the ethereal. Your spirit will benefit from the work you've done, especially the Forgiveness Work because this also releases Karma. This work opens you up to be more connected to Source and what better way to exit than to be walking hand-in-hand with the greatest support system ever.

My advice is to live as if no deadline is pressing and do not be afraid. If your time is coming, then ask for mercy so you will have no fear and be gracious to have been given this opportunity to work on, or with, your body. Your learning is essential to your spiritual growth and evolution as a spiritual being. Continue working on yourself to ease your burdens in life, whether they be physical or emotional. In the end, they are all interlinked—our emotions often being the culprit for the manifestation of our physical issues. It is in our best interests to be mindful of how we show up in the world for ourselves. Working through our traumas and our challenges will alleviate the distress experienced by our body. It truly is a wonder we survive at all given the enormous stressors we put on our body and ourselves.

I hope you have gained some valuable insight and awareness into your relationship with your body and how you can self-heal through the strength of self-belief and the power of your mind. Knowing that you can successfully work through your physical and emotional obstacles and challenges must bring a sense of comfort (if nothing else) because you now have the tools to lighten your load and live your best life. In the end, that's what we all want: to be free from our traumas and our sufferings and to be able to heal our wounds so we can live with freedom. We all deserve this.

Remember, Source is your number one fan. All you need to do is ask with an open heart and mind and let the healing work through you because the Source to all healing truly is within you.

Thank you for your willingness to engage in this book. If it reached out to you and you responded, then it meant you were open to its offerings and for that, I am grateful. I have included some bonus healing procedures that are not necessarily required as part of the Steps to healing your body, but they offer alternative session ideas. So, carry on in your own time to see what else you can apply the healing techniques to and, above all, remember to have fun. Your life may literally depend on it.

~ Disclaimer ~

This book is in no way a medical resource book. The information is not endorsed by the medical profession, nor did I seek endorsement. It is not meant to discourage or replace your engagement in medical treatment or other forms of "regulated" treatment. It is designed only as a companion source to assist you in your healing process. The information encourages and promotes wellness and wellbeing. How you choose to apply this information is entirely up to you. There are NO guarantees that healing will occur or that it is a cure-all. It is not meant to mislead anyone but offer options in alternative ways to assist healing to take place.

Individuals should seek their own medical advice and information before embarking on any alternative methods of healing. This should always be done in the knowledge that you have the free will to choose what is right for you. However, what is recommended to you by a professional should be paramount whenever you are seeking to be fully informed. It is invaluable to your decision making as to how you proceed. In this book, I encourage you to be vigilant in your research and investigations when it comes to any medical or alternative healing methods. It is up to you to do your own research.

If this modality resembles any other modalities already in existence, please note that they may only be similar in either wording chosen or method of application by happenstance, not by deliberate attempt to replicate. It is not meant to reproduce or infringe on any other modalities or be seen as an alternative to any existing method. It is its own method and modality. Any indication that it appears similar is not intentional. It is perhaps that the vocabulary for such spiritual practices is limited, and the words are often collectively used to offer meaning in whatever it is we are trying to relay in simplistic terms, using basic human wording. Often, it is much harder than it appears to find individual interpretation that means the same thing, using unique words that are simply non-existent in today's vocabulary. Spiritual language is not always interpreted well in human language, leaving us reusing words that seem to be borrowed but are not.

I hope that all people will proceed with the greatest care and consideration into their own healing journey.

APPENDIX I
~ Bonus Healing Activations ~

~ Activating Healing Love and Light ~

This is a lovely, simple healing when you just need a boost of **love and light** from **Source**. It's a great little technique if you're feeling down or want an energy recharge, or just to fill yourself up with divine love. You can do this "love and light" healing anytime, either on its own or as an **add-on**, following on from another Step you've completed as a way to finish off the session. If you were to do this, you would just go straight to Source and ask for the **healing love and light** to be activated within you. Once it's done, you disconnect as usual.

Meditation Process—Activating Healing Love and Light

✤ Connect to Source in **Step 1**. Then ask:

"Dear Source, Divine Creator, I ask you to fill me with your healing love and light. Thank you. It is done. It is complete."

✤ Envision the **healing love and light** as a crystalline waterfall, coming down from Source, entering in through the **Crown Chakra** and moving slowly down through your body, as though it is filling an empty vessel.

✤ Allow all your troubles to float away as this beautiful healing love and light fills your body, taking over all the dark spaces within.

✤ Watch as your body responds to the activation of this healing love and light. See how it becomes charged up and feels full and happy. Feel yourself healing.

✤ When you've finished, return to Source and disconnect. Return to your body and complete your disconnection from Earth. Bring awareness to yourself and then the room, and slowly wake up.

~ Retrieving/Returning Soul Fragments ~

Often, when we have broken away from close relationships their residual soul fragments remain attached to us. When we carry other people's soul fragments around, it's like carrying an extra burden or energy siphon, leaving us feeling energetically depleted. It's best to release these soul fragments and send them home as soon as possible, such as following a break-up, especially if they were very challenging relationships. We also leave some of our own soul fragments behind attached to them. Consequently, we can literally have fragments of ourselves attached to people we've let go of all over the place. Therefore, it is important to not only return soul fragments but retrieve our own, or else it may leave us feeling incomplete.

The first time you do a soul **retrieval**, you'll be asking for all of your soul fragments to return en masse. This can be quite amazing to witness when you see them coming from everywhere back home to you. When you do the soul **returning** for the first time, you'll see a lot being released from you too. Once you've done this initial major soul retrieval/return, from then on, you'll just be dealing directly with people in your life as you go forward. If you are doing this exercise regularly, then you won't have so much of a backlog as you did the first time. You'll most likely be focused on the people, or person, in your present time.

For this exercise, we will be asking Source to retrieve all our soul fragments first, then to do a soul fragment **return**. You can do this in one healing session on its own or you can do it following on from your **Forgiveness Work** in **Step 9**. When we retrieve or return those soul fragments, we will ask that they be cleansed in healing white light.

Meditation Process Part 1–Retrieving Soul Fragments

✸ Connect to Source in Step 1. Then ask:

"Dearest Source, Divine Creator, I ask you to retrieve all my residual soul fragments left behind or attached to those in the past. I ask that they be rinsed off and cleansed in healing white light before returning them home to me. Thank you. It is done. It is complete."

✸ Return to the body and witness the **retrieval** take place.

We may see some of the people that the soul fragments were attached to come into view as they are lifted away from them, or we may just see our soul fragments being corralled and sent up to **Source** to be rinsed in the healing white light.

When I do this, I see them floating into view from all different places, being drawn up into the light to be washed off, then returned whole and sparkling back to me, entering through my Crown Chakra and becoming a part of me again.

Allow your soul fragments to come back to you in the way they wish to, making certain they are cleansed, returned whole and healed.

Meditation Process Part 2–Returning Soul Fragments
(Continuing from **Part 1**.)

✸ To do the return, go back up to Source and ask:

"Dearest Source, Divine Creator, I ask that you return all the residual soul fragments belonging to others. Remove them from me, cleanse them in the healing white light and either dissolve them with you or return them to the person they belong to. Thank you. It is done. It is complete."

- ✸ We then witness those soul fragments being extracted and lifted away from us, being sent up to Source to be cleansed in healing white light, and either dissolved or returned to their owners.

NOTE: I often see them dissolved if they have been a very dark energy attachment from that person, or they're returned cleansed and sparkling back to the owner. Again, how those soul fragments wish to leave you and return is up to them. We just facilitate this process by witnessing it, so it is done and complete.

- ✸ When you've finished, return to Source and disconnect. Return to your body and complete your disconnection from Earth. Bring awareness to yourself and then the room, and slowly wake up.

~ Chakra Balancing and Alignment ~

This Chakra balancing and alignment healing session is fantastic for a body reset and energy recharge. It can be a way to attend to your whole body without being specific about, or focusing on, a particular part of your body that may be unwell. If you're feeling a bit run down or your body feels out of sorts, like it's not running at maximum capacity, then this is a lovely way to reconnect to yourself and charge up.

If you are new to **Chakras**[1] and not certain what I'm talking about, "chakra" is the Sanskrit word meaning **wheel** or **disc**, and they are energy points along your body. It is therefore **energy wheels** we will be working with in this Chakra healing activation and regulation. Chakras regulate your energy flow so that you can be in alignment, and they link in with the body's endocrine system—the system that regulates your hormones, moods and development. Mostly, we focus on seven major ones, although there are many minor ones as well. It is the major Chakras that are referred to when we talk about "the Chakra system".

The seven Chakras are:
1. **Root Chakra**, located in the base of the spine/pelvic floor, is represented by the colour **red**. Helping you to feel grounded in your body and regulating your feelings of security and stability, the Root Chakra is the foundation for life. It is all about survival.
2. **Sacral Chakra**, located below the abdomen, is often associated with the sex organs. It is represented by the colour **orange**. Responsible for your sexual and creative energy, the Sacral Chakra can also be associated with your emotions and how you relate to others in the world.
3. **Solar Plexus Chakra**, located in the stomach region, is represented by the colour **yellow**. Responsible for

---

[1] First written about in the Ancient Hindu texts of knowledge called the "Vedas".

your esteem and confidence in self, the Solar Plexus Chakra helps you to feel in control of your life. It is also related to your identity and works in tandem with the Third Eye Chakra for gut instinct and intuition.

4. **Heart Chakra**, located in the centre of your chest close to your heart, is represented by the colour **green** or **pink**. Associated with love, self-love, and how we show love and compassion to the world, the Heart Chakra can also be referred to as the true **brain**, helping us navigate our world in truth through love of ALL. It is also our source of divine connection.
5. **Throat Chakra**, located in the throat, is represented by the colour **blue**. Associated with our ability to communicate verbally, the Throat Chakra is about having a voice and feeling secure to say our piece, speaking our truth.
6. **Third Eye Chakra**, located in the centre of the forehead between our eyes, is represented by the colour **indigo**. Responsible for our intuition and inner sight relating to our imagination, the Third Eye Chakra also works in tandem with our Solar Plexus Chakra.
7. **Crown Chakra**, located at the top of your head in the centre, is represented by the colour **purple** or **white**. While it is your connection to self, others and the Divine Universe, the Crown Chakra is also the doorway or portal to the spiritual and plays a role in your life's purpose.

For optimum energy flow and feeling aligned in life, these all need to be activated and in harmony so that you feel balanced. If the energy in any Chakra is low, you will feel the effect in that part of your body, either physically or emotionally, as an inability to express the characteristics associated with that Chakra. If the energy is overactive, then that Chakra or its characteristics will tend to dominate, so the key is to be balanced.

Please be aware that this is a very simplistic overview on Chakras in order to give you an idea of their importance in your life. If you're interested in understanding Chakras and how they work, there's a wealth of information written about them in books and online. But you don't need to be an expert on them to do the activation and get them regulated again.

When we do this activation, we will work through each Chakra individually, beginning from the base (or Root Chakra) and working our way up through the seven Chakras. We will begin by asking Source to activate and regulate them. We'll also ask that any Chakras requiring extra work come to our attention. We will tune in to see what is happening there and what the message may be that it's trying to tell us. It is the same as asking for the messages from our body part in **Step 4**.

Once we understand the message revealed to us, we can action it or release it, as the case may be, allowing the Chakra to return to a harmonised state. For example, some of us (like me) may have our Heart Chakra not quite balanced, being slow and sluggish. When we tap in to ask, we may be given the message that we need to love ourselves more, or that we need to allow our hearts to open up to receive love again. This is often the case when we've been so heartbroken that we shut our heart down to protect ourselves and will generally affect other Chakras, like the Solar Plexus Chakra because we no longer trust others or feel safe in the world, or it could affect our Sacral Chakra because we are no longer able to express our creativity, or our libido is shut down so we cannot be intimate. By activating our Chakras and acknowledging the messages, we can simultaneously ask for healing on that Chakra too.

Meditation Process—Chakra Balancing and Alignment

❋ Connect to Source in **Step 1**. Then ask:

"Dearest Source, Divine Creator, I ask that my Chakras be activated and rebalanced so the energy will flow through harmoniously. I ask that any Chakras requiring more attention alert me so I may receive the messages they wish to reveal. I ask that healing be done. Thank you. It is done. It is complete."

- ❋ Return to the body bringing your attention to the **Root Chakra** first, working from the bottom up.
- ❋ Visualise a **wheel** with the applicable colour. In this instance, we see a red wheel for the **Root Chakra**.
- ❋ Take notice to see if it is spinning nicely, or if it is slow and sluggish, or too fast. You will get the feel for equilibrium as you practice this more.
- ❋ Activate each Chakra by sending it white light.
- ❋ Witness it lighting up, so it's alive.
- ❋ Ask it to spin in a balanced harmonious way.
- ❋ Witness this happening.
- ❋ Give each Chakra an affirmation related to its positive characteristics. For example, for the Root Chakra you can say, "**I am safe. I am secure. I am grounded.**"

*NOTE: I've included affirmations for each chakra further on.

- ❋ If it's not running too well, ask if it has a message for you and, if so, acknowledge it.
- ❋ Ask for healing around that issue or you can action it after the session, if required.
- ❋ Once complete, move on to the next Chakra, and so on, repeating the same procedure for each one.
- ❋ When you've attended to each of your Chakras and activated them with the white light so they're all spinning beautifully, tell them they're all "lit up like a runway" ready to perform in perfect harmony with the energy flowing through with ease.
- ❋ When you've finished, return to Source and disconnect. Return to your body and complete your disconnection from Earth. Bring awareness to yourself and then the room, and slowly wake up.

Affirmations for each Chakra:

- **Root Chakra**: "I am safe. I am secure. I am grounded."
- **Sacral Chakra**: " I am free to express my creativity. I am connected to my sexual self. I enjoy sex and intimacy."
- **Solar Plexus**: "I am the master of my emotions. I have a strong sense of self in the world. I have a strong inner KNOWING (gut sense). I trust myself."
- **Heart Chakra**: "I am loving of self. I am open to receiving love. I am connected to humanity through compassion. I am divine love. I am connected to ALL."
- **Throat Chakra**: "I am free to express and be heard. I am free to speak my truth."
- **Third Eye Chakra**: "I am clear on who I am. I have clarity in vision to see what is true. I am open to my expanded consciousness. I have strong intuition and inner sight. I see magic in the world."
- **Crown Chakra**: "I am connected to a higher power. I am open to receiving Divine instruction. I am connected to ALL. I am eternal and expansive. I am a Spiritual being."

~ Activate Protective Light Shield ~

At times, we can become susceptible to unwanted and negative energies when we are out in public, or when we are visiting places or people that we may not be comfortable around and perhaps need a little extra protection. This is a simple technique to activate your own personal protective light shield or bubble. I use it freely when heading out into busy public places, or when I'm going to go to visit people who I find a little energetically draining. I may even activate one before clients come, so I am not vulnerable to their energies.

Some options I use are:
- A white light barrier, which gives a great protective field of energy that also transmutes any harmful energies from entering.
- A pink love shield if I wish to emit a protective love energy field.
- For a more heavy-duty shield, one where I am 'invisible' to others, I imagine a very dense, opaque purple bubble surrounding me.

If you like, you can make up your own shield or barrier. Sometimes, they can appear in any form they wish. I've even had them emitting an electric current, or copper coiling to shield me.

Meditation Process–Activating Protective Light Shield
- ❋ Connect with Source in **Step 1**.
- ❋ Ask for a protective shield to be activated:

"Dear Source, Divine Creator, I ask that a protective light shield *(or preferred protective bubble)* be activated. Thank you. It is done. It is complete."

- ❈ Return to your body and watch as the shield or bubble is activated around you.
- ❈ Disconnect from Source and Earth when complete, returning to your body, feeling secure and safe as you go out into the world.

*TIP: You can activate light shields around your home, your car, your pets, your family members, and more. It's the same process. Add it into the **asking** and watch it be actualised.*

Appendix II

- Reading Recommendations and References -

~ Reading Recommendations ~

- Basili, Ann M., 2022, *Astara and Erefrey, Goddesses of the Realm and the Little Blue Planet* (published children's book), Dragonfly Publishing.
- Brock, Ann Graham, 2003, *Mary Magdalene, The First Apostle: The Struggle for Authority*, Harvard Divinity School.
- Cannon, Dolores, 2001-2015, *The Convoluted Universe* (volumes 1-5), Ozark Mountain Publishing.
- Cannon, Dolores, 1998, *The Custodians*, Ozark Mountain Publishing.
- Cannon, Dolores, 1993, *Keepers of the Garden*, Ozark Mountain Publishing.
- Cannon, Julia, 2013, *Soul Speak: The Language of Your Body*, Ozark Mountain Publishing.
- Hay, Louise L., 1985, *You Can Heal Your Life*, Hay House.
- Hicks, Esther and Jerry, 2007, *The Law of Attraction: The Basics of the Teachings of Abraham*, Hay House.
- Hicks, Esther and Jerry, 2004, *Ask and it is Given: Learning to Manifest Your Desires*, Hay House.
- Keys of Enoch (n.d.), *DNA and the Divine Names*, https://keysofenoch.org/dna-and-the-divine-names/, accessed September 2023.
- LeLoup, Jean-Yves, 2002, *The Gospel of Mary Magdalene*, Inner Traditions.
- Morse, Dr Robert, 2004, *The Detox Miracle Sourcebook*, Kalindi Press.
- Newton, Michael, 1994, *Journey of Souls: Case Studies of Life Between Lives*, Llewellyn Publications.
- Robinson, James and Meyer, Marvin (editors), 2009, *The Nag Hammadi Scriptures: The Revised and Updated Translation of Sacred Gnostic Texts*, HarperCollins Publishers.
- Starbird, Margaret, 2003, *Magdalene's Lost Legacy*, Bear & Company.
- Tolle, Eckhart, 1997, *The Power of Now: A Guide to Spiritual Enlightenment*, New World Library.

- Wilson, Stuart and Prentis, Joanna, 2008, *The Power of the Magdalene*, Ozark Mountain Publishing.
- Wilson, Stuart and Prentis, Joanna, 2020, *The Magdalene Version: Secret Wisdom from a Gnostic Mystery School*, Ozark Mountain Publishing.

NOTE: you can also find Esther and Jerry Hicks and Dr Robert Morse on YouTube.

~ References ~

- Cannon, D. (2011) *The Three Waves of Volunteers and the New Earth*, Kindle Edition.
- Cannon, D., n.d., *What is Quantum Healing Hypnosis Technique?* https://www.dolorescannon.com/about-qhht/, accessed September 2023.
- Clow, B. H. (2018) *Revelations of the Aquarian Age*, Bear & Company, United States.
- Clow, B. H. (2011) *Awakening the Planetary Mind*, Inner Traditions, Bear & Company, United States.
- Graham, L. (2016). *Epigenetics and Russia. Proceedings of the American Philosophical Society*, 160(3), 266-271. http://www.jstor.org/stable/26159182
- Hurtak, J. J, (2009) *The Book of Knowledge: The Keys of Enoch - DNA and the Divine Names*, The Academy of Future Science.
- Stibal, Vianna (n.d.), *ThetaHealing*, https://www.thetahealing.com, accessed September 2023.

ACKNOWLEDGMENTS

Thank you, dear Lisa & Mark Wolstenholme, for listening to me talk about my wish to write this book one lazy summer evening in the hills of Perth. With your encouragement to "just write it", I have. Thankyou Lisa, for your friendship, kindness and support. I am so grateful for you.

Thank you, Michelle Smith, for asking much more of me than I thought was possible in order to deliver a far better piece of written work. You were the "eye" required to make sure those with no knowledge of the metaphysical or spiritual could understand what I was saying.

Thank you to my little Earth angel helper, Aura Luna the Pomeranian, who's always by my side offering me companionship & joy.

And finally...
Thank you to Source for being a strong presence of unconditional love in my every day. I find you revealing yourself in so many subtle ways through the trees, ocean, sky and birds. You showed me mercy when I lost my way and gave me the chance to live my life over. In this way I found my purpose - to help others heal and not be afraid of living.

About The Author

Ann Basili lives in the idyllic town of Margaret River, Western Australia. After relocating from the beachside suburbs of Perth to the country, her work as a healer has flourished, as has her writing and creativity. She has found being in the country affords her the lifestyle she has always desired surrounded by nature, peace and harmony. She feels this has inspired her deepening spiritual practices, allowing her healing work to evolve into more of a vocation rather than a profession.

Through her own metamorphosis, she has learned that life is truly for living in wellness and that everyone deserves this experience. She has committed herself to helping heal others through her work as a Quantum Healer, utilising her training as a hypnosis and regression practitioner (QHHT®), Theta Healer, counsellor and spiritual educator. She believes this is the mission she was born for.

Ann's writing has mainly been focused on sharing healing inspiration and stories that ignite a deeper awareness of the world around us. From writing on her social media platforms to publishing a beautiful heartfelt children's book influenced by her love of the Earth, she sees writing as a powerful tool for conveying deep spiritual messages in a way people can understand easily. Her aim is always to take whatever the complex message is and translate it in a way that is simple. She knows this is her gift.

As far as healing goes, she believes the message needs to be simple and accessible in order for people to feel like they can try it, otherwise they're unable to relate to it and sadly, many miss out because the language does not resonate or the concepts are too abstract. So with that in mind, Ann has embarked on translating her healing journey into a writing journey so others can share in and learn from it too.

~~~~~

Ann has Bachelor degrees in Sociology, Anthropology and Social Work. She is a certified Quantum Healing Hypnosis practitioner (QHHT®), Advanced ThetaHealer® and Counsellor with over 25 years' experience working with people. She currently runs her own private healing practice - Orion Metaphysical.

You can find Ann at:

www.annmbasiliauthor.com

or

www.orionmetaphysical.com.au

www.ingramcontent.com/pod-product-compliance
Lightning Source LLC
Chambersburg PA
CBHW020322010526
44107CB00054B/1941